CONFESSIONS OF A
SINISTER MINISTER

DICK HUSER

To order additional copies of this book, contact:
Xlibris Corporation
1-888-795-4274
www.Xlibris.com
Orders@Xlibris.com
20795

CONTENTS

To my Holy Family

BiOGRAPHY

W. Richard (Dick) Huser tells of his journey as student, pastor, life insurance salesman, regional manager, bartender, coffee vendor, business owner, national seminar speaker, professional journal contributor, and once again pastor.

Born and raised in Holdenville, Oklahoma, a graduate of Oklahoma City University and Southern Methodist University, careers in California, travels in Europe, provide unexpected and strange experiences to share with family and friends. These are the "confessions" of his spiritual journey. It is a look behind the veil of organized religion and the personae of pastors and people. Take a look for yourself.

Dick lives with his wife, Arlene, in Sun City, Lincoln Hills, California.

SUMMARY

D ick Huser tells his story of theology schools and mainstream churches from the inside out. It is a story drawn from the raw materials of the human condition. It is a profile of real people who turn to pastors from a myriad of motives. It is the story of his own progress and regress and regeneration, as he struggled with the paradoxical nature of church history, ancient creeds, modern interpretations, and the clash of a dramatically new culture with traditional credos. The vulnerability of his journey is exposed for all to see, and the healing influence of family, friends and colleagues becomes happily apparent.

ACKNOWLEDGEMENTS

First of all, I want to express my gratitude and admiration to my beloved wife, Arlene. She is my ship, my anchor, my keel board, my rudder, and the wind in my sails. All I had was the tiller. Without her encouragement I would never have completed this task.

I am forever grateful for the influence of my four sons. Mark, Stan, Dan, and Damon, each in their own way, have given me insights and revelations I could not have seen had they not been an intimate part of my life. They were more "reality" than I could always cope with, but I wouldn't trade a moment of our adventures together for an easier pathway.

The grandchildren have also helped make life worth living. Will, Natalie, Cherie, Miles and Levi have brought hours of delight and warmth beyond their understanding or imagination. Someday they will know, when it's their turn to reap the harvest.

Robert van der Toorren was the most interesting and challenging friend I have ever known. Rob was artist, architect, musician, engineer, underground soldier (in Holland, during WWII), top ranking Dutch intelligence officer, and raconteur of the first order. His many adventure stories ranged from Holland to Britain to China to the jungles of Java, and all true.

The Nazis marched into Holland in 1939, when Rob was 13 years old. His affluent father had built a hiding place following World War I. Under the carpet, beneath the house, through a tunnel, into a hidden chamber, Rob could go and spend hours teaching himself the violin, how to paint, and several languages with the help of tutors.

The soldiers knew that Rob was "somewhere," through friends of friends, and local connections. They would come by his house, looking for the teenage boy, and shoot helter skelter into the walls, in case he might be hiding there. Rob's revenge took the form of garroting Nazi soldiers in the middle of the night with a wire from his mother's grand piano, and learning not to use too much dynamite on selected targets!

As a young man Rob was enrolled in the University of Leiden, and while studying engineering, law, art, medicine, and architecture, he was assigned as "Commissioner of Consumables," which meant he was in charge of the wine cellars of the University, the most distinguished in Holland. He said all the wine was hidden by separate individuals during the war, and 90% of it returned following the war.

We are privileged to have a few of Rob's art works hanging in our home. It was Rob who gave me the title of this book, though he has been deceased for a number of years. He was a "word dink" of the first order, and we had many a wonderful time together between golf and chess games to play with the English language. It was his creation of what we now call a "frame game" puzzle that triggered my desire to someday use the phrase, the "Sinister Minister."

"FRAME GAME"

IS (s) TER

IS (m) TER

Or: S-in-ISTER   M-in-ISTER   Thus: Sinister Minister

Cancer of the brain took Rob away from us, far too early.

But as Morrie Schwartz said, "Death ends a life, not a relationship." I miss you, Rob.

The late Reverend Noel LeRoque deserves mention here. He helped the "Prodigal Son" come home, and was an extremely good friend, golf companion, and encourager in a hundred ways. He is another one of those exceptionally gifted and multi-talented human beings, author and mosaic artist. Noel designed and made a nameplate mosaic for us. It simply says, "Huser, Arlene and Richard," upside down, and right side up. It's a conversation piece.

Hundreds of members and friends of our churches are additional gifts to our lives. So many cherished times together, so many unexpected pleasures and heartaches, so many blessings and challenges we faced together, so many friendships that stretch over the years. My life is like a patchwork quilt, with each passage being sewn together to form a blanket of purpose that spans my very fortunate life. Sometimes it was a "crazy quilt," but that's life.

I write this for myself. It is great therapy. Like all therapy, it hurts and it helps. I write this for my sons and their families, and my grandchildren. Maybe they can grasp just how truly insane and mysterious their grandfather was. I write this for people who think you have to be "nice" if you are "religious."

We've all heard of "Finding Forrester" and "Finding Nemo." This is "Finding Dick." It is simply a playful and energetic romp through my adventures as well as my misadventures.

Credits go to Chuck Myer and Arthur Howe for assistance in editing. Any "mistrakes" are mine. My heartfelt thanks to my sister-in-law, Yvonne Huser, for the dramatic cover art. She's been a good friend and soulmate forever.

A word about my "dedication." My Holy Family includes my children and grandchildren, and beyond those, my extended, blended, tended and mended family, including a host of splendid friends who make life worthwhile.

As "Nature Boy" said, "The greatest thing you'll ever learn is just to love, and be loved in return."

HEADS UP

"Woe to you, religious leaders. You are like beautiful mausoleums full of dead men's bones, of foulness and corruptions. You try to look like saintly men . . . ."

Matthew 23:27

This book is about sex and about God. It is about pleasure and suffering, beauty and ugliness, fullness and emptiness, "success" and "failure." It is about the spirit and the flesh, heaven and earth, love versus lust, and greed versus grace. Things we all go through.

It is about the adventure of one human spirit in search of awareness. It is the story of a young man who had no idea what was ahead of him. But then, who did?

I have enjoyed a very circuitous journey. I have had a helluva romp as student, pastor, life insurance salesman, bartender, candle maker, coffee vendor, business entrepreneur, national seminar director, mortician (for one day), back to pastoring, and host for a real estate sales team. I have always enjoyed "raising a little hell on the way to heaven."

What is the "secular" life? What is the "sacred" life? I find no difference, since God is everywhere and in all places and events of human life. The psalmist says: "Thank you for making me so wonderfully complex!" (Psalm 139:14)

I was never comfortable being addressed as "Reverend." I found it created more of a barrier than a bridge to advance relationships. If one is introduced as "Pastor" or Reverend, it usually causes people to change their behavior or speech, makes them project their image of what a pastor should be, and makes them show what they think is their "best" side, which may be their worst. Maybe we should be addressed as "Spiritual Coach."

Those "religious" folk who want us all to go out and "save souls" will be disappointed. I never did believe God was dependent upon us to save anyone. That was God's job, and that Being has a very good track record. I have a few letters I have kept over the years from people who credit me for helping God help them and even for saving their lives. I am fully aware that "God works in mysterious ways," and sometimes God used even me to help someone else.

Most "church people" want their pastors to be more saccharine than salty, more "sweet and low" than acerbic and upbeat. St. Paul said all believers are priests. The only "High Priest" I recognize is Jesus. So it's the Reverend You as well as Reverend Me. Get used to it.

Much of what is communicated today in televised "worship services," and in a vast number of growing churches with "contemporary worship" or "entertainment evangelism," I consider spiritual escapism. That is, emotion is substituted for content or substance. "Where's the beef?"

People want to believe, to have an anchor, a rock to cling to, and the "dry bones" of "theological expertise" do not always feed the soul, so they turn to the emotional fix.

The United Methodists do have it right when they balance Scripture with Reason and Experience with Tradition. But somewhere along the way the Passion seems to have subsided. It's hard to balance the "Social Gospel" with the "Evangelical Urge," and the "Rational Appeal" with "Religious Tradition."

Religion seems to separate folks, while Spirituality can bring us together. Religion usually stinks. Spirituality usually sparkles. But each can enhance the other, and seem to need each other. The more "religious" people are, the less spiritual health and integrity they exhibit as a rule.

I hope this offends many, for then I believe I am on the right track. Who was it that said, "Today's truth is yesterday's heresy?" I know it was Huxley who said, "It is the customary fate of new truths to begin as heresies and to end as superstitions."

So my "truth" will no doubt be absorbed into the great black hole of the future, and tossed into the dumpster of all other books of wisdom and knowledge.

My beloved wife tells me that this presentation a bit "raw." She's usually right. But then, life is raw, and that's the plain, down to earth result I want. God works, I find, in and from and through the raw materials of our lives.

This epic or opusculum is not as raw as it could be. I have pulled a few punches in the spirit of some discretion.

I have a lot of quarrels with the church, but the "church" has been good to me. And may I suggest I might have been a little good for the church. Even in my down times I did not turn to the Conference to subsidize my counseling or "periods of disability," as some did and do. I did help out in the establishment of churches and church buildings that were not in existence before I came along, and resuscitated a gasping historical church.

I am extremely grateful for the checkered passages in my life. I write this to remember and to touch on significant episodes. Pastors are all too human, and that tends to frustrate the world of the churched and non-churched. Find in it what you will, it was my experience, my challenge, and my road to fulfillment. Who knows, this might help you find yours.

CHAPTER 1

PILLOW

EROS

"Your teeth are white as sheep's wool, newly shorn and washed; perfectly matched, without one missing."

Song of Solomon 4:2 (TLB)

Her name was Pillow. No it wasn't, but it was close enough, and had the same stirring effect on my gonads. Her name was a distraction; let alone her svelte figure and sensuous countenance. I was a quietly raging 26 year old pastor in the late 1950's, fresh out of seminary at Southern Methodist University, Perkins School of Theology, filled with passion: for ministry, for my new surroundings (Monterey Peninsula), for social distinction, for advancement, for knowledge of the "real world," and just a plain old *joie de vie*.

I also coveted most of the seven deadly sins: lust, envy, pride, greed, etc. I was at war with myself, but seemed to be enjoying it

21

thoroughly. My spiritual quest was deep but clouded, and my earthly quest was to make a mark and love doing it.

When I arrived in Monterey, the little "starter cell" of a new church was meeting in a small Mortuary chapel. I usually preached over a casket to about 20 pilgrims. We outgrew that space in about a year, and moved on to the too large but comfortable USO building.

In the fourth year of my ministry, we had managed to gather enough folks and funding to build our chapel on Carmel Hill in Monterey, at the intersection of Soledad and Pacific, just above "Motel Row" on Highway One. By this time we were a well-established presence on the Peninsula, and many new and young families, many of them military, helped to strengthen and prosper our new church.

One fine day I made a pastoral call on a "new" family. They lived in a little apartment near the church. He was a businessman, and she sat at home all day wondering what to do with all of the passion that she said surged inside her all the time. She tells her pastor that right off the bat! Especially if he is young, eager, and wondering inside why he has many of the same thoughts, and how is he supposed to minister to this young firefly.

Pillow tells me she has a lover in San Jose, and she is going to meet him next week. She is attracted to him because he has great teeth! She can't resist his teeth. I begin to wonder about my teeth.

She wants me to do my first miracle. She wants me to pray for her next Wednesday afternoon at three when she's going to meet him, so that she will have the inner strength to resist his advances. Sure she does. She's on fire, always on fire, but she wants me to put out the fire with my prayers. No problem! This is one of many of my pastoral challenges.

Now I'm eager to be of assistance in any way possible, so next Wednesday at three, I'm in my church office, praying for Pillow. She, on the other hand, is on a different channel, in San Jose. She's relishing the moment. So I keep praying while she keeps doing whatever she and he are doing. I am doing the Lord's work, and I'm confident I can make a difference. I can hardly wait for the report.

When I see her next week, in my study, alone together, I am filled with restraint and a pastor's heart of compassion and hope for her healing. I ask how it went. She said it went very, very well. They had a marvelous "afternoon delight." She was sooo ashamed, but sooo satisfied. She could hardly wait to fail her next test.

How could I have failed? Why she was taking another kind of delight in telling me all this, and giving me all those furtive glances, and making these impossible requests of me, and I'm so young and dumb, that even though I know all about Paul Tillich and "The Courage to Be," I'm vulnerable in her presence? No, we didn't do it. I was still a true disciple of Paul who went to great lengths to remind me this was not a good thing.

I remembered Mark Twain's quips that he could resist anything but temptation, and that the only temptations he ever regretted were the ones he didn't yield to. I wondered if I shared that outlook. I remembered my lawyer father's favorite line from a musical: "Brother, you can't be put in jail for what you're thinkin'!"

About a year later Pillow slipped me a note on her way out of the church service. It was a short note. She said that drinking from my passion would be like having communion with Jesus, and that it must have been the way Mary and Martha felt. Now I had read Emil Brunner's thousand page "Divine Imperative," but this was a different imperative altogether.

St. Paul said it was better to marry than to burn, but that made no sense for I was married and I was still a raging furnace. The famed theologian Reinhold Niebuhr said it was sometimes impossible to know whether you were being a "fool for Christ" as St. Paul claimed, or just a damned fool! I had an idea which one I was. As Joseph Campbell said to Bill Moyers, it's credo vs. libido, all the way.

St. John's Gospel said the Word was made Flesh, so I was still trying to sort out the flesh from the Word, and discern the difference, and how one united with the other. I know that Ideas precede Reality. Reality gives birth to new ideas. I was having ideas.

Somehow the concept of "sublimation" didn't seem to be doing the job entirely, but I kept very busy at church and civic work, sermon preparation and family outings. I was elected President of the Monterey Kiwanis Club in 1959, and was nominated "Man of the Year" by the Monterey Peninsula Junior Chamber of Commerce.

As chairman of the Monterey Peninsula Committee on Alcoholism, I was sent to Yale University for a month to study the syndrome. I learned about the chemical content of wine vs. beer vs. spirits, and the emotional and physical addictions to alcohol. I learned at Yale what someone called "Positive Addictions" to offset the other forces of gravity in our lives. One of the female colleagues offered herself to me as a "positive addiction."

Well, I had my own gravity working on me. I began to think I had better get out of the pastoral ministry before I screwed up my family, the church family, and made a miserable mess of what had been, up to now, a fine success story. Things were rather lackluster at home, (no blame intended,) so I was far too vulnerable and susceptible to the parade of opportunities that presented themselves to me almost every day in the many social arenas in which I was involved.

I would not have been the first to fall prey to basic instincts. Bishops, pastors, professors, politicians, evangelists, medical doctors, psychiatrists, plumbers, all are vulnerable. Will power does not always function effectively.

We are all wired differently. Some of us are 110, some 220, and some 440, or 880, and maybe more. People do the darnedest things, and we should expect the unexplainable, because it happens all the time. That goes for libido, id, IQ, ego, and whatever other equipment we are given at birth.

We can't all be Mother Teresas, or the human race would cease to exist. The media stories are always about how pastors seduce innocent parishioners, but *Au Contraire!* Most of the time we are fending them off.

The myth is that we professionals have all the power, but may I suggest that the flock or the clients have powers of their very own. And they love to use them with impunity, in all arenas of human life. I think the pastor is perceived as a "safe target" for those who want to expand their sensual or political or social outreach, and I've know a few pastors who were the unfortunate targets of those agendas.

Another striking female entity showed her teeth to me, and then gave me a book by the great Jesuit Scholar, Pierre Teilhard de Chardin, "The Phenomenon of Man," and informed me that my faith was rather naïve, and I should go home and read the rest of the Song of Solomon, and perhaps I would grow up some day, and let her have her way with me. So I did. Which do you think I did?

Solomon's Song was already surfing through my soul, and my will power was wilting and waning away. I was hell-bent for what my church called "continuing education," so I did more reading. I read the life of Frank Harris, a thoroughly sexual romp, and that seemed to be an appealing kind of research. I now knew how King David was moved, looking over the balcony down to the sensuous Bathsheba. I wasn't ready to kill for it, like he did. But I was ready.

I saw Pillow some 30 years later, and she whispered to me in a reception line, "It never did stop, Dick." I guess a little Eros goes a long, long way. I can only imagine that her quest for the "silver chalice" never ended. She was chasing a myth.

There were absolutely no classes on these things in seminary. Sometimes I tried to recall the theological controversy over the difference between the "*homoousion*" (God really in the flesh of Jesus) and the "*homoiousion*" (or God in Jesus incarnate with mirrors). I did remember how the Arian "heresy" (Jesus as a natural man) almost displaced the Athanasian "truth" (Jesus as a supernatural intervention) but it seemed irrelevant at this point. Athanasius won the debate by a slim margin, but Will Durant and Harry Overstreet thought Arius was right. Life, they said, was not about salvation, but maturity.

In the third century the homosexual issue was still deeply embedded in the closet, so that the agony and ecstasy was all over the homoousion deal. One of the ancients said he could never believe that God was once a burping baby! Therefore the *"iousions"* had it all over the *"ousions."* Oh, the power of one tiny "i". This was heady stuff! But what did it have to do with a young theology graduate wrestling with the needs of suffering people, social upheaval, and his own inward quest?

So the die was cast. What should I do, having retired from the pastoral ministry at the mature age of 30? Well, with two degrees in theology, why not sell life insurance? "There's no man with endurance, like the man who sells insurance." So began the next ten years of my spiritual adventure. But I'm way ahead of myself.

CHAPTER 2

FLASHBACK

CHRONOS

"My son, listen to me and do as I say, and you
will have a long, good life."

Proverbs 4:10 (TLB)

I was a "spoiled child," so I was told, in that I was the youngest
of four kids, the happy recipient of a hobbyhorse, a pedal car,
a tricycle, a wagon with sideboards, a scooter, roller skates, and a
bike. All in delirious sequence.

A few words about my hometown, Holdenville. I suppose
one could take a dart and throw it at a map of our fair land, and
still not find a better place in which to be born and raised. Of
course, it wasn't near the ocean or the mountains, but outside of
those gaps it was very nice. I didn't notice the difference. San
Francisco sounded like a faraway land.

It was a world of ragweed, "stickers," rattlesnakes, armadillos,
muddy rivers, quicksand, cottonmouths (water moccasins), dust

storms, tornadoes, chiggers, and other environmental amenities of central Oklahoma.

It was also the site of "lightning bugs," four leaf clovers, small vegetable gardens, good schools, nurturing Sunday Schools, and many social and cultural delights, productive farms, prosperous ranches, and, yes, oil fields.

Children could play safely in the back yard: "Annie Over," "Ally, Ally, Oxen Free," kick the can, leapfrog, red rover, Piggy wants a motion, capture the flag, rubber gun fights (a favorite). Those were the days when tire inner tubes were made of rubber, and, when discarded, were considered trash by gas stations. Their trash was our treasure. Cut into huge rubber bands, stretched over one to three foot board "guns," secured by clothespins, these weapons could sting the "enemy," and climax in great victories.

Alleys behind houses provided sanctuary for mischief, and short cuts through neighborhoods. We could run or ride bikes for miles around town without any sense of fear or danger. No one knew where we were, or had any concerns. The dumpsters in the alleys behind stores held vast treasures for young boys, such as bottle tops with cork interiors that could lock onto your shirt for display and bragging rights.

Young boys could go into the fields on the edge of town and have real (dirt) clod fights. One could get hurt or lose an eye, but we knew that wouldn't happen to us. Sword fights with wooden swords was fun but bruising. Nearby lakes offered frog stabbing or shooting, crawdad and perch fishing, overnight camping, and absorbed young and blissful hours.

The local swimming pool was of generous design, and offered hours and hours of summer sunshine and high diving proficiency. The pool was located next to the inviting "Stroup Park," an oasis for kids to roam and play. Fortunately Yvonne Huser, my talented sister-in-law, was eventually appointed "Park Commissioner," and she designed and installed walking paths and encouraged the planting of trees along the way.

A nickel went a long way in those days. My early boyhood days were during the Depression, though I didn't know it. Dad was a small town lawyer, struggling to provide a home and raise four children. He learned all about the existential abyss without any philosophical gurus. He thought psychiatry was a bunch of crap, and, if you could figure out yourself, you knew the other guy was going through the same thing.

Dad was self-educated, and brilliant in his own way. Dad loved words, history, music, humor, literature, poetry (Bobby Burns "For A' That"), public speaking, and imprinted that love on me. When he won a "civil" lawsuit, after a convincing argument, he would come home and dance a "jig" on our linoleum floor in the kitchen. Once in a while he would play his old fiddle. Dad loved life.

Mom, too, was gifted and intelligent. She had graduated from the same law school as Dad, which is how they met. She taught herself to play the grand organ in the church in a grand fashion, pulling out combinations of the 20 "stops," going from one manual to another, with very fancy footwork on the pedals. And she could bake a cake!

At home we had many harmonious family hours singing from an old songbook. Mom played the piano, while Dad would sing his favorites: "Out on the Deep," (showing off his bass voice), "My Heart's In The Highlands," "In The Gloaming," and songs of the sea, like "Nancy Lee." He had been a Navy Yeoman in World War I.

Mom excelled in bridge playing. She was not above pitching in when times were hard, and became a seamstress for a fine dress shop to help carry the awesome load. She loved to crochet and knit, and we still have beautiful Afghans she knitted, even after her stroke left one hand paralyzed.

Once in a while Mom would have help from "colored town" come in. There was "Bee" (for Beola), Mozelle, and others who taught me how to help with the laundry. We used four tubs: one for washing (a soap tub), then a rinse tub, then a tub for bluing, and another rinse tub. We fed the clothes through the ringer which swung around and over each tub, and that was the most fun part. Hanging the clothes on a line finished the job.

Our family doctor, Dr. Wallace called me "Tough-enough-stuff!" It was his way of saying "this won't hurt" when he gave you a shot, or cut into you. He once diagnosed me as having some kind of rash, and he gave Mom an ointment to administer that burned like the living fires of hell upon application, which Mom liberally applied from hips down and shoulders outward "for my own good."

After about 20 days of this infernal torture, the good Dr. changed his mind. It was only impetigo, and the new medicine was like a soothing cream, and all the distressed sores evaporated. Dr. Wallace loved tonsillectomies, so he performed four of them on me: too high, too low, not enough, one more. Lots of ice cream was my reward for his lack of skill.

Then there was Dr. Hicks, the nose and throat ogre. He screwed long metal screws up each nostril, let them drain, and then took a suction device to my nose and asked me to say "kay, kay, kay" so that the suction would work, and out came the stuff he thought he was curing. It was gory and stupid and ineffective. All I really had was a runny nose from allergies, but nobody knew it then. The doctor's "high tech" treatments were ridiculous, but he had a nice house.

My hobbies included model airplane building with balsa wood and lots of glue (before sniffing was in). Making and flying kites was thrilling. Stringing beads for belts and key chains and bookmarks took time. Playing marbles was great, until you got to playing "keepsies," then you lost your marbles, and it was a very bad day. Mumblety-peg was super, unless you stabbed yourself. We had lots of do-it-yourself pastimes, like yo-yo's and spinning tops, and, the greatest of all, a Lionel train set with switch tracks.

One of our outdoor sports was on a flat board chassis with two-by-two board axles, and small ball-bearing "wheels" (more filling station trash) attached to the end of each. The steering wheel was one small rope tied to each end of the front axle. We would have races down the little used surface streets (concrete). I was way too little, but was encouraged by my older brothers to give it a try.

One summer evening at sunset I set off on my "maiden voyage". Ahead of me came a Model-T, head on, driven by a teenager, and it may have been his first solo outing, also. I tried to turn away from his path, and so did the driver. We turned into each other, and he ran over me. Fortunately, it was a lightweight vehicle with something like bicycle tires. I remember looking up into the engine upon contact, and saw real, or imagined, fire. I was thrown to the curb, and was unconscious for a half hour or more. I was not hospitalized, but the incident may serve to explain the rest of my life.

I went on to take piano lessons for six years. My first teacher was a stunning Greek goddess by the name of Jenny. She was a real beauty, and I could hardly wait to get my 8-year old ass over to her house and sit next to her on the bench for my weekly lessons. She was a favorite student of a famed piano professor at Oklahoma City University, so I was chosen to be a part of a troupe of young kids for a concert in the City. We played "Tales from the Vienna Woods."

At first they sat me in the rear of the vast stage, but then, without notice, I was moved with a young lady to the very front, and seated at an enormous grand piano. Hallelujah! I think the Dean of Music liked Jenny, so he favored her students.

Fireworks on the Fourth of July were a completely different story when I was young. There were few restrictions. We could buy cherry bombs, fountains, torpedoes, Roman candles, skyrockets, sparklers, and other more dangerous weapons. It was the kind of thing you could lose fingers or hands with, or put out your eyes forever, but it was fun.

A young pal of mine and I climbed the elm tree in my front yard one day. The branches hung out over the highway below. We were armed with 22 shells. We thought it would be fun to throw them down on the pavement below, to see if we could set one off. After about the fourth try, we succeeded. A bullet whizzed by our ears to our complete astonishment. We abandoned the experiment.

We went back to slingshots. We killed robins and sparrows

and other helpless creatures. It was basic instinct. A Daisy Air Rifle improved our deadliness. We were part of the balance of nature.

I kept on wetting the bed until I was twelve, and even had a mishap when I was the guest of a college fraternity just before high school graduation. It was a wonderful feeling waking up wet and warm and smelling like a urinal.

Another dangerous mission was to ride on our bikes down to the railroad trestle, put our ears on the track, and wait for an oncoming train. We could crawl right up into the infrastructure of the wooden bridge, so that we could actually feel the weight of the million-ton locomotive roar over us just a few inches above as the wooden beams bent down perilously close to our backsides. How many kids got to do that?

Holdenville was special, in that we had two railroad lines intersecting just below Main Street: the "Rock Island Line," and the "Frisco Line." The Rock Island ran from Memphis to Amarillo, and the train was a sleek sight to behold.

When my sister-in-law, Yvonne, was about 14 years of age, she was invited to christen the "Choctaw Rocket" in Oklahoma City, because she was a Choctaw Princess. The Mayor, the Governor, and the Choctaw Chief himself were all present to see "Princess Pale Moon" break the bottle on the engine's nose. It was big, very big. My Dad enjoyed repeating the story of the conductor of the train. After a brief stopover in Holdenville, the black conductor would stand in uniform by the steps of the passenger car, and announce in a big, booming voice: "All aboard for Wewoka Seminole Shawnee Oklahoma City and ooon and oon!" Maybe he was the first rapper.

The local cotton gin offered friendly diversion. My middle brother Ernie and I were allowed to climb the high structure that held the sorting belt, and jump far down below into the cotton hulls. One day the ultimate treat was offered us. We could jump right down into the pure cotton, before it was baled. What a nice, soft-landing that would be. It was. Ernie disappeared! With muffled cries he shouted for help. I don't remember how they got him out, but he lives and prospers today.

In the summer time a "Liniment Show" would come to town. They set up a stage on the edge of town by the swimming pool. It included a "minstrel show," with an "interlocutor" and two "end men." Then there was this guy with no shirt on, who could suck up his stomach until you could see his backbone.

I went home and practiced that, and got close. If you're skin and bones like I was, it helps. They sold a lot of bottles of liniment, which could cure anything. Bottles and dollars were flying back and forth in the excitement. They knew what they were doing. This was real, down-home, live, sweaty entertainment.

I did get to clean the chicken-coop once in a while, and admire the bravery of my father who would catch and wring a chicken's neck, so Mom could boil and pluck the feathers and I could eat the neck and the heart and the gizzard and liver and all my favorite pieces!

My oldest brother Stanley initiated me into the "Royal Order of Siam." You get down on your knees, crouch onto the carpet, lift your arms now and then, and say the magic words: "Oh-wah-tah-goo-siam." Say it faster and faster till you caught on. He introduced me to other stupid games, too, all at my expense. That was a big brother's job. My job was to wonder why. That was one of the perks of being "spoiled." After all, he owned a "zoot suit," a large key chain, and had everything but hand-me-downs.

Sister Kathryn, second in line, was a talented girl, who spent hours and hours of frustration at the piano, thanks to Mom's insistence. She grew up and into a beautiful mother of three. She passed away not long ago.

But for now, life was good.

CHAPTER 3

ADOLESCENT AGONY

CRAZOS

"David met Jonathan, the king's son, and there
was an immediate bond of love between them.
Jonathan swore to be his blood brother, and sealed
the pact by giving him his robe, sword, bow,
and belt."

(1 Samuel 18)

Adolescence is a critical period for the best of us. Hormones
and hunger and health and happiness and holiness and hopes
and heartbreaks and hell raisin' and new hair and horniness all
collide on a grand scale in the stadium of our burgeoning souls.

I was a scrawny little anemic kid, who grew up to be the only
asthmatic Drum Major of a High School Band in Oklahoma.
It's very hard to signal a marching band when you don't have
enough wind to breathe, let alone blow the whistle! But I did it.

I was an enterprising boy. I'm not sure in which order, but I sold magazines door to door, rode a horse-drawn milk wagon and carted bottles to front doors, cut lawns with a push mower, hacked weeds with a hand sickle, shined shoes at the local shoe store, clerked at the five-and-dime store (and cleaned toilets), stocked the shelves, sold popcorn at the local theatres, delivered newspapers, worked for a wholesale tobacco and candy distributor, pumped gasoline at a "filling station," sold "Marvel Mystery Oil," fixed flats and lubed cars, drove used cars to other dealers, handed out political flyers in neighborhoods, collected coat hangers to sell back to the dry cleaners, set pins at the local bowling alley, and many other "odd jobs."

I was even hired on as a clerk in the Court Clerk's office, and typed a bunch of stuff for actual legal cases and documents, and learned a little legalese. It was a tiny taste of my father's profession.

The psychological environment was something else. This was a town of about 5,000 souls, which it still is today. The times have changed for the better, like the rest of the country, but when I grew up, there was a lot of prejudice in the air. Beneath all the smiling faces was an understanding of who was "in," and who was "out." Southern hospitality was not all-inclusive. (Actually, that's true everywhere.)

I don't know why, but I always knew better. So in a small town, there were selective folks we could associate with. I guess we were the aristocrats, or the "stupid white people," depending on your point of view.

One evening my parents were sitting on the front porch, and Dad was reminiscing about how fortunate he was, and how grateful he was to have come out of the Depression and landing on both feet. He said something like this: "We have a nice house, and good neighbors on our block. There's the Hasketts, and the Hahns, and the Holmes, and the Halls, (at this point, a light came on in his mind) and the Husers. We live on Hinckley Street, in Holdenville, in Hughes County." He paused a moment: "Is this Heaven or Hell?"

I was eventually denied the companionship of a young man named Harold. He was a few years older, but we enjoyed collecting stamps together on Sunday afternoons, and comparing finds. One day my father said I was not to go over to his house anymore. Why? I had no idea. And I was not brave enough to ask. As I look back over it, I think my parents thought he was "a queer." I would not have understood anyway.

The summer days were filled with biking and camping and fishing. We would dry corn-silk and roll and smoke it, until we were able to finagle a way to stash some Prince Albert tobacco in our back packs, and roll Bull Durham or Bugle and chew "Brown's Mule" or something else in a can that tasted horrible, but was very man-building. We were told all this would "stunt your growth," along with other dangerous boyhood habits. You know.

The Cub Scouts and Boy Scouts gave me goals to shoot for. So I raced through Bobcat, Wolf, and Bear, on to the rank of Lion with Gold and Silver arrows. In Boy Scouts I started from Tenderfoot and soared on through the merit badge hurdles to finally become an Eagle Scout.

I enjoyed going backpacking with my Scout Troop, and learned to burn eggs and Spam out in the open, thrive on "Vienna Sausages," and slap at bugs. I was surviving the traumatic teens.

Then the older scouts introduced us to a strange rite of passage. We were to go down to the park next to the cemetery, make a campfire, listen to the scoutmaster tell us ghost stories, and then, trembling, crawl over the railroad tracks and journey through the cemetery.

No problem. I sat there through about five frightful stories, while the boys were picked, one by one, to begin their trek through the graveyard. They promised us it would be well marked, and we couldn't get confused as to which direction to find the trail. We knew there would be some ghastly surprises that were prepared for us.

Suddenly it was my turn. I crept away from the campfire, crawled over the railroad tracks that were mounted on a high levy, crawled down on the other side, and stole silently away. Not toward the cemetery. I was homeward bound. I was sooo ashamed, but soooo glad to still be alive!

I had often thought back to that moment of cowardice and complete humiliation, until I read an episode in the life of Franklin D. Roosevelt. He too, had an embarrassing moment while he was a student at Harvard. Running to catch a train, he knocked down a small Italian boy coming out of an alley.

The boy went down and began bawling. The neighbors began to gather, and Roosevelt tried to calm the boy by handing him a dollar. But it looked like he was taking the dollar away from the boy. In panic, he fled, leading a large crowd in close pursuit, and barely caught the next train, with the help of a brakeman, out of town.

It was a great comfort to me to know that even the high and mighty have humiliating moments. FDR's name is on my Eagle Scout certificate. I still have all my badges and stuff. My oldest brother Stanley, having returned from WWII, completed his tasks in Scouting and we were pinned Eagles together.

You could go hunting for rabbit, quail, and squirrel. My father bought me a "410" double barrel shotgun. It was a beauty, a classic, which I failed to appreciate fully. When I went to college, I went to a pawnshop and traded it in for an old clunker of a typewriter, much to the chagrin of my Dad. But I needed a different weapon if I was to continue my "higher education." I'm sure my Dad would have found a better way to acquire the typewriter if I had given him the chance.

I was allergic to reading, so my "book reports" in high school were gleaned from Classic Comics. I was even allergic to movies. For Mom to send me off to a movie was a form of punishment. Until one fine day there was a movie with Ginger Rogers and Fred Astaire, a musical, and I was hooked for life. I did see "Song of Bernadette," and came away wondering what the "Immaculate Conception" was. I asked the mother of a "girl friend," but she referred me to Mom, who referred me to Dad, and I got nowhere.

My High School teachers were first class. The teachers of vocal and band music were really in tune with the kids, and brought forth music from the students they didn't know was within them. English, drama, shop, American history, Spanish, algebra, all good stuff, and well presented. I remember mastering the art of whistling through my teeth, to the consternation of one of my teachers, who would stop and look at us one at a time, and never (fortunately) nailed me as the culprit.

All through high school I lived a life of envy and anger and frustration. All my grade school male friends had grown into muscles and masculinity, while I had barely pubed.

Looking out the windows at grade school and high school, I wondered and waited and wished, daydreaming of great things to come, things that always seemed completely out of reach. It was "survival of the fittest," and I was the "97 pound weakling" that Charles Atlas talked about.

I seemed to be allergic to everything on the whole earth, so while the other boys dated cheerleaders, I searched for a nice, good-looking girl that was as desperate as I was for companionship, who didn't mind if I wheezed and my nose ran all the time and when I found one I treated her so badly and told her I didn't want to "go steady" anymore on the phone, and for the next two years I wanted to be with her more than anyone else although she would have absolutely nothing to do with me.

One summer I was sent off to "Boy's State," a camp designed to instruct young teenagers about the political process. We studied parties and elections, municipal and county government, the executive and judicial departments, and held elections at different levels throughout the week. I was elected "City Treasurer," but that's as far as I got in the statewide infrastructure.

I did "count coup" on one level. I managed to sidle up to the Major of the quasi-national guard, and became "Regimental Adjutant." The whole camp was divided into companies and battalions, and reported up the ranks to me, Top Dog. What it really meant was that I got to be first in the chow line every day, at every meal. That was better than an elective office.

Every Saturday night I hitchhiked (no problem then) to another small town in Oklahoma about 30 miles away with my slide trombone to play in a western jazz band in the American

Legion Hall and sing "I Don't Know Why," and search for my first true love. Nothing came of that. Nothing came of anything.

One of the great thrills was to be a part of a small band at a Rodeo. Five of us were mounted with our instruments on a platform right above the gates where the wild horses and bulls were released. When the gates opened we played "Hold That Tiger," and I would enjoy the glory of sliding my trombone at the entry of each musical phrase. We were there three full days, and almost starved to death, saved only by candy bars.

My biggest challenge at age 14 was trying to breathe, while my brother Stanley was in Europe, a P-38fighter pilot in the Army Air Corps at age 22, shooting down German planes and dropping thousand pound bombs and strafing trains and railroads and convoys. He was handsome and smart and brave and true and funny and strong and clever and knitted sweaters and socks and scarves back at his barracks and played poker in between killing Nazis. I would never be a man like him and come home all decorated and into the arms of the most beautiful and talented girl I had ever seen and become a lawyer like my dad and always do everything perfectly. He was my hero. Still is.

I did become a page boy in the State Senate at age 14, thanks to my father's law partner who was a Senator. It was a great thrill to wander around the halls and shout at the top of my lungs, "Paging Senator Snodgrass!" I was carrying a little paper note from someone who wanted to reach the Senator, and I was sure to get a tip of a quarter or half dollar. That was our pay. It was huge.

I could toss the half dollar straight up into the dome high above me, and catch it before it bounced on the granite floors. Then I was over to the second floor, where a blind host would man the refreshment counter. He always recognized me (and everyone else) by some unknown clue. It was the best job I ever had.

I proved a small measure of manhood by scaling the massive granite walls of the State Capitol Building in Oklahoma City, without benefit of Nikes or Adidas. I think they were Buster Browns, with leather soles.

As I looked down from the third floor exterior wall of the capitol, clinging desperately to the ridges between the granite blocks, I noticed the wrought iron fence that surrounded the capitol. There were spear-like tops on the all the fence bars looking straight up at me and in the grip of total fear I knew I could not climb down but only up.

I needed an Invisible Hand with a firm grasp. Fortunately, I had a companion. A friend of mine was on the ledge above, and reached down with a strong hand and pulled me up out of danger. This was another of many "close calls" in my life.

One day a western band came to play on the radio in downtown Oklahoma City. I played hooky from my job at the State Senate, and took a bus to the radio station to hear the band live, and on the air. It was a great thrill. Upon my return that afternoon to the Capitol, my father was waiting. It was the one day he had chosen to visit his famous son, and I was AWOL. That was my final day at the State Senate, and the ride home with Dad was a very silent and tense two hours. I was back to school the next day.

There was not much to do on those hot summer nights in a little town in Oklahoma, so we had to create our diversions. One of them offered a temptation too hard to resist. By this time we lived on a hill on a highway close to downtown, and my father, struggling as he was financially, owned an old Ford (1936 I believe). He parked his car on the shoulder of the highway in front of our house, facing down hill. This Ford had no key, simply an ignition switch. You took off the brake, put in the clutch, let the car start rolling down the hill, turn on the ignition, let the clutch out slowly, and "Eureka," the motor would turn over, and you were on your way to anywhere.

A high school chum would sometimes spend the night with me. Ours was a two-story house. We would wait downstairs until my parents went to bed, make sure the front door was not locked, and then slowly climb the stairs to our bedroom, counting the stairs to mark which ones squeaked. Our bedroom faced the neighbor's house and garden. They were always growing something, which meant the ground was soft and furrowed. A bay window on the first floor beneath the bedroom gave us a small roof to climb down on, and a large crepe myrtle provided a semblance of a ladder until we could jump safely into the neighbor's field.

We would silently steal away into the night, hoping to gain some research on what God hath made, and we would like to. My pal had the edge on me, as he already had a special girl friend, and they had lived the dream many times. She had a girl friend, and with persistent encouragement she consented to give it a try.

Where is the perfect place to try? My chum was the custodian of a church, with keys. So he had the "keys to the kingdom." We entered the sanctuary (which means a safe place), and they occupied one pew, and we another, several rows apart. Thanks to ignorance, fear, guilt, and a very narrow pew, I was a dismal failure. The phrases "performance anxiety" or "erectile dysfunction" had not yet been coined, but perhaps I was a pioneer in the field. Maybe the ambience had something to do with it.

I suppose the "sinister side" of my character was being formed in these little getaways. Our return to my house was eagerly anticipated. We revved up the Ford until we were in coasting range, turned off the motor and the headlights, and coasted silently back to the front of the house. Carefully opening the front door, we maneuvered the staircase ritual all over again, and breathed a tremendous sigh of relief when we slipped under the covers, and see who could fart the best, or belch the longest. Of course we were crazy. What did you expect? We were David and Jonathan, who also dreamed the impossible.

It was during these years that I finally had some kind of physical awakening, so I had to postpone myself in the privacy of my bedroom until I could manage the real thing, and dreaded the time another opportunity presented itself.

My buddy had let it be known that he was the proud owner of only one testicle, and so we began to call him "Ace." It must have served him well, for in addition to his many conquests, he was gifted with a deep, resonant bass voice, which won him many titles at state singing competitions. Maybe baritones have two balls, and tenors three or four.

I did attempt to play a trombone solo once at the annual High School Band Concert. It was to be "Stormy Weather." It was. After three notes my mouth turned into cotton and I couldn't produce another sound and I left the stage in total humiliation and ran home took refuge under the covers. It was another episode in a completely happy childhood.

Music saved my adolescent sanity. I was selected to sing with the High School Boy's Quartet, and we performed often at local and state levels. Music was to prove a healing and inspirational dynamic in all the days to come. Between concerts and dramatic plays, I discovered I liked the stage a lot.

In our early teens a few of us were shipped off to church camp. There were few other diversions, as the latest in technology was a radio, a "swamp cooler," a sewing machine and a vacuum sweeper. So here was I, hungry for some kind of meaning in life.

I found it in a little brush arbor in a remote campground in Oklahoma. Two young firebrand pastors asked me if I loved Jesus, the Jesus they had so persuasively presented, and at age 15 I decided that Jesus was the only Guy I could ever really love, trust, and follow, if what they said was true.

So when they gave "the altar call," I felt an Invisible Presence in my senses, and up I crawled on the sawdust, and poured out my little virginal heart, and confessed all two of my sins, (ignorance and mischief) and dedicated my life to God. Even as a boy my heart knew something my mind would have yet to comprehend. I had not yet read Blaise Pascal, who said, *"The heart has its reasons which reason knows nothing of."*

When the counselor came into the dormitory that night, and sat by my cot to encourage me, I told him that I was sure that God wanted me to serve in a very "special way," but I had no idea what that meant. He was a good man. The specials all came later in life.

I learned all the "old hymns," beauties like, "There Is a Fountain Filled With Blood, Drawn From Immanuel's Veins!" It was gross, but I didn't get it, so it didn't matter. Fear and guilt, Jesus and Satan, the dynamic duos of Bible Belt Christianity, took hold of me by the scruff of the neck, and held me fast to my course. "Love Lifted Me" came later.

Welcome to Christianity! Welcome to The Methodist Church! At age 16 I made an appointment with the pastor of the Holdenville Methodist Church. He received me warmly, as I, unknowingly, would prove to be a "feather in his cap." After hearing of my intention to enter the ministry, he gave me some very curious advice. "The first thing you should do, Richard, is to buy the Bishop a hat! (A nice, felt Fedora!)" That would jumpstart my career in the Oklahoma Conference, Big Time. It was not a very informative or inspirational interview, and I began to wonder what on earth I had gotten myself into.

My first sermon at age 16 was preached in a black church. It was located "on the other side of the tracks," but they had got word that a new young preacher boy was in the making. So they invited me to preach to them. I don't know what I said, but every other sentence was followed by a loud "amen!" It served mainly to shake me up, but I knew they were trying to encourage me all the way. In white churches the people sit in quiet desperation no matter what the preacher says.

The black pastor had a fine introduction for me. He said, "This young man has decided to become a preacher. Praise the Lord! And his father is a lawyer! Now ain't that amazin'!" I guess it was. Amen!

When I graduated from High School, I was presented with the "Danforth Foundation Award for Leadership!" I was totally caught off guard, as I believed a football star would be receiving that one. The award was a book by Danforth, "I Dare You." It began by saying that if I was to amount to something, I should dare to do the daring. "Break a window," do something, get with it. I suppose that's why I broke a few windows (of opportunity) all along life's merry way.

All in all, it was a sweet little town, the place where I was born and raised, and I still think of it as "Holy Ground." My hometown is still sacred to me. When I visit I love to drive around the side streets and alleys and Main Street, and just reminisce.

> *"O little town of Holdenville*
> *How still we see thee lie.*
> *Above thy deep and dreamless sleep*
> *The silent stars go by."*

That song could be sung of any hamlet in the world at eventide.

> *"Yet in thy dark streets shineth*
> *The everlasting light . . . ."*
>> For all who have eyes to see.
>> And angel's song, for all those who have ears
> to hear.

> *"The hopes and fears of all the years*
> *Are met in thee tonight."*

CHAPTER 4

NAUGHTY MARIETTA

PHILOS

"Praise Him with the trumpet (& trombone)
Praise Him with stringed instruments & horns.
Psalm 150:4-5 (TLB)

B unny was her name. Really. But I never got close. She was an amazing soprano, and sang the lead in all the musicals. Every man wanted Bunny, but she was too good for any man. I wanted to design a "T Shirt" for her that said "I Like You," on the front, and on the back it would say, "But You Don't Qualify!"

My college days were full of fun and frolic, except for my ill-advised decision to "pledge" into a fraternity. The "initiation ceremony," when you went from pledge to brother, was transparent. I could see right through it, and my "brothers" never forgave me for not "breaking down" during the infantile ritual of passage from "pledge" to "brother." There never was a brotherhood, but simply an ongoing hazing by the older and wiser 1945 veterans who had returned from the WWII, and enjoyed spoofing the young college kids.

I was appointed to serve a couple of little country churches 80 miles from Oklahoma City University. My first "church" was a handful of farmers who met in a country schoolhouse. My pay was whatever was in the offering plate, as we had no other expenses. Four or five dollars was a big offering.

Then I was assigned to real little churches in small bus stop hamlets, and that was my traffic path on weekends. I washed dishes for my board at the frat house and worked in a bank after school to support my scholastic endeavors.

I learned very little about the Bible in college from a geriatric prof who always played with the middle button of his suit coat during his stand-up lectures. He almost completely buttoned it one time, but not quite. This geriatric professor loved to quote some famous evangelist who always began his "revival" meetings with this thunderbolt: "Will all of the ladies in the audience please cross your legs? Now that the gates of hell are closed, we can continue!"

Then it was over to comparative religions, logic, philosophy, drama, and art appreciation, while I played trombone in the college band and the symphony orchestra and the marching band and sang in musicals like "Naughty Marietta" (starring Bunny) and acted in plays like "Our Town" and I began dating.

A few of the "pre-ministerial" students got together and formed what we called the "Sky Pilots." We met once a week. That's all we did. We just met. We were not like John Wesley's "Holy Club" who met, but also went out and did good works. One day we had an epiphany. Frank Laubach, who had been a missionary in an Asian country for years, visited us. He was working on developing a universal language.

Laubach introduced us to his little pamphlet called "The Game With Minutes." The idea was to attempt to think of God at least once in each minute of the day. It was a real challenge for me. It was another of my failures.

One of the college girls I dated did not suffer from "arousal dysfunction." On our first date she got me out on her front porch at night and proceeded to explain to me how one of her breasts was bigger than the other and wouldn't I like to see the difference and why would I stop there and what a stupid young preacher boy I really was and she would never see me again! I had failed her game with minutes.

Another young lady offered herself to me after several dates. About three seconds before my engine coupled with her caboose, she asked if I really loved her this much! My pre-ministerial veins were bursting with honesty, if not chastity, and I retreated from my destination, and drove home from Tulsa wondering just what it was I really wanted from life. I guess I was suffering from "delayed adolescence."

After the blitz of intellectual and carnal and artistic and social research during the week, I would hitchhike down to my appointed rural churches and hitchhike back to campus. Before long I was able to buy a 1941 Chevy four-door sedan. Black. I was a man, with spunk, spizzerinktum, gumption, and wheels. I preached. Some of the sermons were kind of my own. Most were do-overs from sermon books, but then I knew absolutely nothing about preaching.

Once in a while, as the tiny congregation sang, I would have to cover my face with the hymnbook. The little flock had long since divided up the parts they would sing, and when a little old farmer reached his high tenor part, and floated the note for all to admire, it was all I could do to contain myself.

One fine day the famous tenor, James Melton of the International Harvester Hour, brought his weekly radio show to Oklahoma City University. I was selected among eleven other voices to back him up, and there I was, on the radio, heard all across America!

College life was good, thanks to music and art and drama, and my car. No beer drinking. I was still a good boy, and that was not easy. It was during the college days that I met and married the very fine young lady who became the wonderful mother of three of my sons: an Oklahoman, a Texan, and a Californian. Those stories come later on.

The summer times were spent as a counselor at a YMCA camp for boys. We sang "Found a Peanut", "Leprosy", "John Brown's Body", "Clementine", "Vas Is Das Here", "Sippin' Cider", "Web Footed Friends", "Marching to the Gallows", "She Climbed Into the Water", and other innocuous camp songs, that seemed to assuage the luncheon frenzy before compulsory nap time. Those were halcyon days, and many good friends were made beyond my usual circles.

CHAPTER 5

THE GAUNTLET

LOGOS

"Beware of these experts in religion, for they love
to parade in dignified robes and to be bowed to by
the people as they walk along the street. Even while
they are praying long prayers with great outward
piety, they are planning schemes."
Jesus of Nazareth: Luke 20:46-47

One of the ancients said that faith without reason was blind,
and reason without faith was empty. Well, I was empty
and blind, so I was a perfect candidate for a theological seminary,
at age 22. A college graduate, maybe I knew a little something.

Perkins School of Theology on the campus of Southern
Methodist University looked like a palatial, gilt-edged compound.
With the chapel rising in the center of the campus, the halls of
learning and the living quarters were bold red brick edifices,

framed by white columns and filigree. It was new, pristine and impressive. It was an immaculate conception.

The shaping of mind and soul is a sensitive business. The professors at theological seminaries are "masters of the universe." They were the generals, training the foot soldiers who would go out on the front lines, and face the enemy. If I thought initiation into a fraternity was tough, it was child's play compared to my initiation into the world of the abstruse and eclectic wisdom of the ages.

In high school, I took "shop." It was woodworking, learning how to use all the tools, and avoid losing fingers. My favorite tool was the lathe. You could take a two-by-two, or a four-by-four, and turn that sucker into a lamp-post, or a totem pole, or anything your heart desired. Now I was that four-by-four on the lathe, and the sculptors had their shaping cutters all ready for me, long before my arrival.

On a practical level, I was most fortunate. When I first visited Perkins School of Theology, I needed a home for my family of one wife and one child. It was suggested to me to go to the matron of "Hawk Hall." She was searching for a manager of the "married with children" apartments. They were brand new, very nice, and the ideal place to live during the graduate days. She had unusual perception, so she "hired" me for the job. Free rent was my compensation. Three years of this was a huge assist. I became "House Mother" for about thirty families, and helped trouble shoot any problems with each unit.

Back to the quest for truth. In seminary we had a real firebrand professor by the name of Joe Mathews who was anti-everything that the church had ever stood for, and pro-something most seminarians could never fathom.

He once asked the question in his ethics class: "Now you all know what happens if you have too much sex, don't you?" Total silence. We hadn't a clue. "Boredom!" he shouted. "Bore me," we all thought to ourselves. It would be kind of like having Robert De Niro in a vengeful role as a theology professor. He was hip and mean and came at you like a sawed off shotgun with a rich mixture of philosophy and drama and psychology and art and literature and all made into a stir fry that you were supposed to swallow whole and go forth and do likewise.

You didn't dare sit on the front row. Joe might hit you! He did once, to a poor lad who asked how God speaks to us. With harmless blows of an eraser about his head and shoulders our Teacher demonstrated this, and said, "That's how God speaks to us!"

Joe said we would never amount to anything until we knew the Bible so well that we could call Abraham, Isaac, and Jacob: Abe, Ike, and Jake! Get to know them on a first name basis. So we went on to Joe and Moe. And now Prof Joe Mathews is simply Joe, and Dr. Albert Outler is Al.

Prof Joe liked the hard stuff, the rough stuff, like the art of Rouault and Picasso, and the music of Stravinsky, especially the "Rite of Spring." We sat for an hour listening to the most discordant movement while Joe grimaced and emoted and displayed the ecstasy of the total agony for the benefit of all of his sycophants. Then he made sure we read the novels of Kafka and Camus and their crowd, the philosophy of Heidegger and Kant, the theology of Karl Barth and Paul Tillich. He wanted us to read the "Tough Guys" so that we would learn how to swim upstream with the sharks.

Joe didn't like balance. He liked things tilting; he liked radical departures, the critical mass. Joe saw the Gospel in the movie, "The Barefoot Contessa," in which Ava Gardner made the discovery that she had married an impotent man. No wonder she went nuts! I guess that's the kind of "upagainstness" that the Gospel was talking about. Joe didn't want us to miss the point.

Joe was a prophet and an iconoclast, confronting all the false gods of theology and psychology and philosophy and culture and religion, and whatever else remained standing that had not yet been reduced to ashes so we could start the world all over again. It was because he had been a chaplain during WWII, and had seen men get their heads blown off, and had put his hand in the "goo" that was once his buddy's face.

Joe warned us that too simplistic an approach to theology

was nothing less than spiritual masturbation! He was scary! It was as if he had prescience about the coming of "entertainment evangelism."

"God is a sonofabitch . . . . but he loves you!" was his punch line. Gee, I could hardly wait to use that line on my first flock. God uses all the negativity in your life to get your attention. The more the challenges, the more God loves you.

Joe listened to neglected wives of "cold" seminarians who were too busy with their studies, and then admonished his all male students (in those days) to go home and "be animals with your wives for the glory of God." Joe also suggested that politicians were lying "for the glory of God." Everything was for the glory of God! When Joseph Stalin died, Joe said that Stalin was a great man. He said it twice, but I guess I just don't understand Joe's definition of greatness.

"Glub, glub, glub," you may be going down for the third time, and that's when you will understand just how existential God really is, when you give up every rational and emotional and psychological approach you ever had in understanding your spiritual ass!

Boy, this was fun! Everything with Joe was "utterly," and ness, ness, ness. My lostness, my confusionness, my seminariness, my ignoranceness. Especially my upagainstness! That's where God was going to meet me, in the great abyss of the mind and soul, and I could hardly wait to get down there to my utterness!

Dr. Albert Outler provided the Yin for Prof. Joe Mathews' Yang, and I was the Yo-Yo in between. These "master baiters" had me going and coming, torn between their bait and switch lectures. My soul was being yanked out of its socket and shoved back in again.

Al employed the completely rational approach to all that was necessary for the complete training of a young preacher. Dr. Outler knew all languages, all theologies, all philosophies, all religions, all psychological schools, all political systems, all histories, all arts, all musics, all dramatic plays, all of the all of all.

One fine spring day in his Systematic Theology Lecture, Al

proclaimed to his large class, in an effort to provide balance to those of us who had been swindled by Prof. Joe's neo-orthodox theological spell, that "Objectivity cannot prove its own omniscience, and subjectivity cannot prove its own omniscience!" Hallelujah!

Wow! I thought to myself, we seminary students will surely be able to use THAT on our future flocks. So I said right out loud an AMEN in the middle of the class! Nobody had ever done that before to Outler, or any other Prof. Al responded by uttering something about the student who shouldn't show too much enthusiasm for either one of those "tivities" or isms.

I had a private audience with Joe, and told him about Al's pronouncement on Objectivity and Subjectivity. His response? "Precisely! That's why truth IS subjective!" And then he added, "Mr. Huser, did you tell him (Al) that?" I suppose I was to be the middleman between these two giants. Maybe the "Pontiff," which means bridge.

I went to visit Al in his study, which was filled with the odor of incense and I knew I was in the presence of the Holy Angel of Truth. He could tell I was under the spell of Prof. Joe, so he suggested Bach's Brandenburg Concertos as an antidote to Stravinsky, Monet as a cure for Chagall, and Thomas Aquinas as an immunization against Sartre.

I told Albert I had an invitation from the one and only great theater director Margo Jones who was holding forth at Dallas' very famous "Theatre in the Round" and who had offered me a part in one of her productions. I remember being in her spacious hotel suite, stepping over scripts scattered over the floor, and reacting to her dramatic manner of sizing me up.

Dr. Outler said it would be a tragic mistake if I accepted a part, as it would complicate my studies and diminish my devotion to my calling, let alone screw up my weekend schedules with my country church just above the border in Oklahoma. So I took his advice and it probably saved my life, but I hated him for it. "I could have been a contender."

So we were caught in the crossfire of two very intelligent

professors: one a liberal rationalist, and the other a neo-orthodox existentialist. It was a bit much for an uninformed product of an Oklahoma Bible camp to absorb in a moment. But as much as I may protest, it was a kick in the pants for a young student who had finally decided to apply himself and hit the books.

I tried to reconcile these two irresistible forces and immovable professors with my final term paper, which I decided to submit to each prof *in exacta*, and see the response in the grading psychology of each.

My term paper was simply "A Critique and Appraisal of the Doctrine of the Incarnation and Atonement as Seen in Two Works of Soren Kierkegaard: 'The Fragments,' and 'The Postscript.'" What a wonderful thing to know! It was really a kind of re-visitation of the *homoousion* controversy, in which I insisted that Jesus Christ was fully God, and fully man, and how God had pulled it off.

What I did was to attempt to reconcile Kierkegaard's "Vertical Moment" with Socrates' "Horizontal Maieuticism." My solution was the "breakthrough" concept of convergence. The premise was that the divine converged with the human, and eternity converged with time. If matter issued from spirit, then it was subject to it, like water carving out the Grand Canyon.

So I stated rhetorically that it was the fusion of the Kierkegaardian "Moment" with the Socratic "Occasion" that reconciled the reality of God becoming Man, and thus the awesome and paradoxical tension was finally resolved in the carrel of an SMU theology library. It was an eclectic and erudite epiphany. These were the times of Revelation, and the seals were broken. The world has never been the same since. HALLELUJAH!

I turned this masterpiece in for my final term paper to both Al and Joe. It was a brilliant stroke that saved me a lot of homework time, but it proved to be a little mistake, in that Joe didn't like it at all, and graded me a B-, which caused me to graduate "without honors," by a slight decimal of a grade average.

I appealed to Joe, to no avail. Neo-orthodoxy was, at last, quite rigid. Joe didn't like me "dissing" his hero, Soren K.

I got a grade "A" from Prof Al, the rational prof, who knew a great thing when he read it. He loved it and told another student that I was some kind of genius! Well, that was better than the dog-gone Honor Roll! I knew that most geniuses were all screwed up, so that would explain a lot of things as I went through life. As the musical sang, "Oh it's nice to be a genius, of course, but keep that ol' horse before the cart . . . you gotta have heart."

Dr. Al's remarks at the end of the term paper included the perception that I "tend to go at people (authors, and others) as if to hack and maim," which I guess I still do, partly in jest, partly to wake up, and partly to question the validity of remarks, just to make sure there's no phoniness going on. My Dad hated hypocrisy, and of course the world is full of it. That's how we all get along.

At the end of the day, Joe told one of my colleagues that I had stayed one year too long in seminary. I had gone down the rationalist drain. I guess I was really ripe for the "picki'n" at the end of two years, but Al had spoiled me with abstruse errors and esoteric theories in the last year. Joe didn't like deserters from his cause.

The very odd thing is that I have kept that term paper in my filing cabinet for almost 50 years! It is turning yellow, as if into parchment. When I scan it again it is astonishing to see how much I used to know, and how little I could ever use from the pulpit. But it was the high point of my formal education.

They should have called seminary "The Butcher Shop," because if you still believed in God by the time you finished your third graduate year, you were some kind of stir-fry instead of the standing rib or rump roast you went in as. You sure as hell didn't believe in the same God you took to SMU. But you had read Kafka's Metamorphosis, and you could hardly wait to go out into the world and minister to all of Franz's cockroaches who couldn't possibly turn back into human beings because they were utterly in their "lostness"! I could have written a book: "I'm a Cockroach, You're a Cockroach." It would have made better sense than the "I'm OK" book.

I don't suppose that Perkins School of Theology is that much different than all the other seminaries of all the other "mainstream" denominations. Most lay people haven't the foggiest what their pastors have studied. Most perceive that we have simply spent our time memorizing the Bible, basking in church history, or maybe taking guitar lessons.

I received recently a journal from another theology school. They have a new professor, and among his "merit badges" he is said to be a panentheist, and a proponent of a theology that is "hypothetical, dialogical, and pluralistic." Just the thing young seminarians and local church folk need in order to reclaim their souls and head for the Promised Land.

It's beginning to look like the philosophers have outwitted the theologians, and are winning the day. At least, in the mainstream theology schools. My virginal beliefs were surgically removed, and the vacuum was immediately filled with an abundant skepticism, open philosophical hungers, artistic appreciation, and lust for life. I didn't appreciate it completely at the time, but seminary saved me from "being saved."

I was set to become a Maverick Methodist Minister. It would just be a matter of time and opportunity. The love of Jesus was secure in my soul. Nothing had come along that surpassed the Sermon on the Mount, or the plain parables about people who were down in the world, but up in God's Mind. Jesus seemed to despise "religion" and religious people. Sallman's "Head of Christ" was way too bland, and could never serve as an image of my Holy Guy/God again.

I should have been more like the young Billy Graham who just went out into the woods and screamed at the trees about the Infallibility of the Bible and the Utter Consequences of rejecting Jesus. But I was studying the E (Elohist) Document and the J (Jehovist) Document and the Q (Quelle) Document and learning the fragmented accumulated speculative relative questionable approach to the Scriptures, like Martin Luther who doubted that the Book of James ever belonged in the New Testament at all.

Even Billy Graham eventually said he should have read more and talked less. Graham wrote that he had been baptized three times: three different immersions, going completely under water, and emerging as a new creature in Christ. Which baptism saved him I don't know, and he didn't say.

I had a close college friend who, with his wife, a few years later had gone to a "Crusade" of Graham's and had his soul "saved". He was one of the official "conversions" of the campaign. He was a wealthy young man, thanks to his father's business acumen, and "had it all."

Then he took a trip to Las Vegas, and had the pleasure of a "massage" from a "masseur". "Bob" privately told me about it. He said he loved it when that guy "rammed that thing in me." He was obviously "converted" by this homosexual encounter. A few months later, he committed suicide, much to the dismay of his wife and family and friends. His newly discovered sexual orientation, quite culturally taboo in those days, had driven him to destroy himself. "Conversions" without content can be of little value in times of crisis. Had he been born a generation later, he would have simply changed churches.

Peter Cartwright, the early American Methodist "Circuit Rider," wrote in his autobiography in the early 1800's that he had confronted a Baptist preacher who had gone around "wetting the jackets" of poor Methodist and Presbyterian souls. Cartwright said that Baptists tried to get to heaven under water, while the Methodists preferred the road to heaven on dry land! Cartwright said that unbaptized babies belonged to heaven just as much as waterlogged grownups.

Cartwright came down hard on the Baptists, who seemed in his eyes to be denying children entrance into heaven, because they had not been immersed, nor reached "the age of accountability."

Well, thanks to my higher education I now had a New Testament that was a compilation of fragments of letters and sayings and episodes from the growing "churches" that were formed around the small world of the first Christians. There were the traditions from the "patriarchates" in Alexandria, Antioch, Moscow, Rome, and others. No Pope yet.

Some of the letters of Paul are now suspect as to their authenticity, and the "Gospel According to Matthew" was really "The Gospel Attributed To Matthew," et al. The "according to" was a way to honor the saints, the huge saints. These clarifications were called "higher criticism," and these refinements were in search of the low down truth.

Nowadays, thanks to the "Jesus Seminar," even the Gospel of John is suspect. A group of eclectic scholars and pastors has appointed itself "guardian" of the truth, and once again reduced the biblical offerings available to us. "Demythologizing" the Bible has become quite a parlor game. Active and retired pastors have monthly lunches and laugh and chat about the naiveté of most Christians, lay and clerical. To paraphrase Paul Simon: "God bless you please, pastor Robinson, Jesus loves you more than you will know. Ho, ho, ho."

A couple of times I would escape from the study carrel in the library at night, and sneak off in my metallic green four-door DeSoto to downtown Dallas, where Candy Barr was holding court as the most infamous stripper in the Southwest, and eventually in the nation, because Carol Doda hadn't yet been invented in San Francisco. While watching Candy I learned to appreciate the female anatomy in a whole new light, and listened, while the M.C. comedian, who was the spitting image of the dean of our seminary, held forth about "Jack & Jill," and how they liked to "fetch." I wondered why God had created so few girls who looked like Candy, and so many of the others, and why I should have ever ended up in Dallas to learn more about Jesus and Paul and St. Augustine who must have had a terrible time himself with his lust and who wrote about it in his Confessions.

Many have appreciated Augustine's full-hearted prayer: "God, Grant me chastity, but not yet! For I was afraid lest Thou shouldst hear me too soon, too soon cure me of my disease of lust, which I desired to have satisfied, rather than extinguished!" He must have been a real Hound Dog! And Jonathan Edwards' "Hound of Heaven" was chasing after him. He left his "wife" (Significant Other) and child to seek holiness. Maybe I should, too.

I read the same scripture St. Augustine read when it changed his life, but it had little or no effect on me. I was already being a good boy. I wasn't doing the things that Augustine had done. I wasn't drinking or smoking or saying "damn" or sleeping around or anything. I was avoiding all the taboos that were expected of young seminary aspirants. But I did "know" that my Prof Joe was nuts if he thought that I could ever get bored with Candy as long as I lived.

I admired what was called "Wesleyan Theology." But I had questions. How could we apply 18th century wisdom to solve 20st century challenges? "Blood" sermons and hymns always left me cold. It always makes more sense to me that it is Jesus' love that heals and redeems us, not his blood. Will and Ariel Durant suggested that the theology of St. Paul had beat out the simple sayings of Jesus about forgiveness and gentle hearts.

"Live and Let Die" is the cold perception of those who have been "saved." The fact that the rest of the world was going to St. Paul's hell was pococurante to the true Bible Believer, because God said it was OK.

It seemed to me now that all ground was "Holy Ground," all mothers are "holy mothers," and all births are "virgin births." Can you look into the face of any newborn child and think of sin? There are many "bastards" who turn out to be quite holy persons, and many legitimate offspring who turn out to be bastards. The Divine Paradox is difficult to comprehend. All of life is holy, even if all people are not. The "Immaculate Conception" turned out to be so much applesauce.

Picture a small group of friends strolling down the street. One is Catholic, another Mormon, and another Methodist. Through the fate of circumstances they have become fast friends. They don't talk religion. They "love one another." Now put them in church. Suddenly there is division, disagreement, tension. These dynamics come as a gift from the hierarchy of each of their religious authorities. Suddenly the friendship is breached, the bonds tested, and the love is conditional. "We just don't talk about it."

Theologians are like meteorologists: they are usually wrong, but the weather is still there, and we have to talk about it. So theologians and scholars are always in error, but the Spirit is still there, and they have to talk about it, and seek the "Truth," always in process.

The "Doppler radar" of even the best of scholars can lead to erroneous predictions. Jesus' little utterance is still true: "The wind blows this way and that. You hear it rustling through the trees, but you have no idea where it comes from or where it's headed next. That's the way it is with everyone 'born from above' by the wind of God, the Spirit of God." (John 3:8) Windy profs and windy evangelists are still blowin' in the wind.

I am truly grateful for the seminary education I processed. It was not like "Bible Schools" that force-feed a literal slant on all scripture. Anything can be proven by the "proof text" method, and "reading into" scripture is just as tricky as "reading out of" scripture. Interpreting the Bible from its historical and biblical context is called *"exegesis."* On the other hand, taking premises into the Bible and using your own ideas to interpret scripture is called *"eisegesis."* Most professors and lay people do the latter, even though they don't know the Greek for it.

Today the growing churches are all obsessed with "end times." It's good business. It's big business. It makes for great evangelistic TV and fad books. It can scare you to death if you're "not ready." God only knows when that will be, but Jesus clearly said "last days" were none of our business, and that "today's troubles" offer enough to keep us occupied.

So it's *exegesis vs. eisegesis*, Sunday morning "Bible Football," depending on which TV channel you choose, and we poor lay people have to discern what the hell is going on. So far, *eisegesis* is winning.

I think of Camus who said, "I shall tell you a great secret, my friend. Do not wait for the last judgment. It takes place every day."

CHAPTER 6

THE APPRENTICE

DUMBOS

"The race is not always to the swift, nor the battle
to the strong . . . .
Nor grace to the learned. Sooner or later bad luck
hits us all . . .
Like fish caught in a cruel net or birds in a trap."
(Ecclesiastes 9:11-12)

They called Oklahoma a "dry state" when I was growing up, but it was always wet enough to "drown your sorrows away." If you were a male Methodist or Baptist or Presbyterian, you had to have "Three things, yea four . . ." as the Good Book would say: a barber, a banker, a butcher, and a bootlegger. Bible toters and bootleggers were strange bedfellows. Neither of them wanted to legalize booze. "Under the table, please."

Women had their basics: a beautician, a bridge partner, a Bible "circle," and a baby sitter. And of course, bargains. "High Society" usually happened in someone's home, with card tables, bridge cards, ashtrays, cigars, cigarettes, sodas, and some other beverage not quite apparent to the kids, and, to be fair, not always served. Quilting was a high priority, and, in times just a little earlier, dresses were made from the pretty prints of flour sacks!

Churches in our town were huge, brick castles. At least they looked that way to the children growing up in them. Outside of Oklahoma City and Tulsa, and a few smaller "cities," the state was sprinkled with small villages. Each of these little hamlets had more than their share of churches. Baptists and Methodists, Presbyterians and Pentecostals had the lion's share, but there were little independent "glory be" churches squeezed in between.

These villages supported a grocery store or two, a couple of "filling stations," a hardware store, and maybe even a clothing store. They were "bus stops," most of them, and how they survived and what they did for entertainment and education was beyond me, unless they just drove to the next town and did research. Like the Camelot song, "What do the simple folk do?"

Meanwhile, in my real world, I was a weekend pastor for small country churches in Oklahoma, just above the Texas border, in order to pay my bills as a student at S.M.U.

I served two years of my three on a "circuit," in Bokchito and Bennington, Oklahoma. Each weekend I would abandon my dormitory family and drive in my DeSoto to the tiny parsonage and begin preparations for Sunday morning and evening services.

Mice skittering across the ancient linoleum flooring accompanied nights spent in this little hovel. Saturday nights were most helpful in my sermon prep, as a country music band inspired the locals to dance the night away, and the dance hall was a mere half block away from my "study."

Days were spent in visitation of farm folk and small town business people, just getting to know them, and welcoming them to church. They were the "salt of the earth." Farmers, merchants, widows and struggling pilgrims of every kind, wondering how to react to this young man who was on his way to God knew where.

I recall visiting Sam, a lonely pilgrim in his seventies, living in a one-room shack about one block behind "Main Street," which was the highway running through town. I was 22 years of age, and this was one scary moment for me. The man didn't scare me. The location didn't scare me. The smell, the poverty, and the plight of the old man did. I tried to play "cool," but I'm sure he saw right through me. I tried to "minister" to him, and invited him to church. But I never saw him again, nor really wanted to.

After a few months, the town fathers approached me to be "Justice of the Peace." "Judge Huser" had a nice ring to it, but my District Superintendent turned thumbs down on the idea. (He was just getting warmed up in putting me down, but I had no idea.)

My prophetic moment came on "Race Relations Sunday." I had invited a young black student by the name of Cecil to come and preach to us, and thus demonstrate our openness to cultural change in the Southwest. I had taken the trouble to obtain permission for this event by consulting the "Official Board" of the church. They knew he was black, and that he was of a different "race."

Cecil and I had become friends while traveling on the bus with the "Seminary Singers" of Perkins Theology School. As we toured the southwest, Cecil and I were paired together to sleep in various homes of willing southerners. The bus was not always allowed to stop at cafes along the way, so we had to keep on rolling until we could find folk who would feed a troupe of singers with two black students on board. It wasn't easy.

A couple of weeks before Race Relations Day arrived, my District Superintendent called me at SMU, and asked me to stop by the District Parsonage on my way to my churches next weekend. My, I thought, what an honor!

When I arrived at the big house, I was ushered into his living room. "Richard, I understand you have invited a colored man to preach in your churches on Race Relations Day! How could you have done such a thing? There are good, honest people who come to your church, and contribute generously to your budget. They are totally offended by your actions."

I tried to explain that I had previous consent from the Official Board. "Well, there has been another meeting of the Official Board, and they are outraged, and will not tolerate this kind of behavior! I don't know where you will be serving a church in the coming year (my last in seminary), but it won't be in my district!" Ouch! I was caught "like a bird in a trap." (I didn't know there was an undercover Official Board. First lesson learned. Powerbrokers are everywhere.)

When I arrived at the parsonage, I found a hate letter stuck in the door. It went on and on about how I had the gall to invite a "nigger," and how the flock was in an uproar over my actions. So, being the young "prophet" that I was, I stood up and read the letter to the congregation on Sunday morning, knowing that someone would surely back me up. But it was not to be.

I was in the process of learning that "practical Christianity" was radically different from "theological Christianity." I'm sure the monks and nuns in the Dark Ages had similar wake-up calls. I was living in another kind of "dark age," but I had no idea what was really going on.

I had the sad task of informing Cecil that he would not be welcome at my churches. I doubt that he was completely surprised. He was, after all, one of the first two "token" black students at SMU, breaking ground for interracial acceptance on campus.

I didn't know I had been "sleeping with a giant" on the Seminary Singers road, but this was Cecil Williams (later of Glide Memorial, San Francisco fame) who hadn't yet climbed the beanstalk.

I managed to land a job as an "Education Director" at another nearby church to help fund me through my last year in seminary. There I ran smack into more hypocrisy and priggish church folk. This same bigoted atmosphere accounted for my eagerness to transfer to get out of town. From my experience with the powers that were in the Oklahoma Conference, I knew one thing for sure. Happiness would be Oklahoma and Texas "in my rear view mirror."

A most fortuitous event manifested itself in the appearance

of Bishop Tippett of the Northern California Conference, who was making a swing through Methodist seminaries recruiting pastors for his territory. We had a brief interview, and in a few days he called me with an invitation to come to California. I told him of my preference to start a church "from scratch." He agreed, and I soon learned that my challenge would be on the Monterey Peninsula. Monterey, California! Hallelujah! I had been delivered from the Southwest, and the suffocating cultural undertones, the "Chamber Music" of disguised bigotry.

I looked up Monterey in the Encyclopedia Britannica. It described Monterey as a quaint, Portuguese fishing village, and mentioned a few other inaccurate phrases, and I wondered what language I would have to learn if I was to serve.

So I sang a little ditty to myself: "Gonna go to California, gonna go to Monterey, sit on the beach and play all day, come-a ty-yie-yippie, yippie yea." Little did I know that yippie would soon be hippie, then yuppy. But that was all to come. The West Coast was calling me, big time.

Before I left theology school, I managed to cross over into the main campus of SMU, and audition in the University's drama department for the Thornton Wilder play, "A Sleep of Prisoners." Four soldiers in wartime, stuck in a chapel in Europe, groping with the meaning of life.

I landed a part, and enjoyed a very satisfying episode of my post-graduate life. "Affairs are now soul size. We have to take the longest stride of faith that man ever took!" Something like that was my big punch line. I was ready for a "long stride of faith."

I was in my very own Sleep, and I was Prisoner of a thousand urges and mystical emotions.

Many years later we were on a cruise of the Aegean/Mediterranean seas. As in most cruises, we were unknowingly programmed to buy something right away, when we were flush. So we ended up in a "hotel" in downtown Istanbul, which was almost completely occupied by carpetbaggers. How could you possibly visit the East without purchasing an expensive and rare silk carpet?

We were all seated around the perimeters of a large hotel

room, provided with sodas or wine or whatever we wished. From out of nowhere we were treated to the charismatic presence of a guy who could have been a "heavy" in the mob, or on the TV show, the "Sopranos."

A half-dozen muscular brutes backed him up, each of whom was in charge of a dozen rolls of exotic and precious carpets. They had a way of hooting and snapping the rolls of carpet as they rolled them out, one by one, in front of us, in oriental splendor. The punch line was the question, "How many knots per square inch do you think there are in this carpet?" We began with a mere 200 knots per square inch. We worked our way up to 1200 knots per square inch. And then the great disclosure: the really special carpets were woven together with "double knots!"

So the revelations all came together. Socrates and Kierkegaard and the Word made flesh and the silk made exquisite . . . time once again converging with eternity. How could we not lay out $5,000 to $10,000 per five foot runner of the purest of carpets in downtown Istanbul on the second day of our tour? We didn't, but a lot of our fellow pilgrims did.

When we got home we bought a carpet runner from Sears for the front door entry . . . . I hadn't the foggiest how many knots there were per square inch. But it looks and works great . . . . and I don't have to worry about people walking on a $5,000 carpet when they come in the front door! That's the kind of theology I wanted to learn . . . . but the profs I had were rather like carpetbaggers whose flim-flam was hard to decipher. They were "hard closers."

Martin Luther had written against the doctrine of "Transubstantiation," the concept being when you served "mass" or communion and blessed the elements, the wafer became, in fact, the body of Christ, and the wine, in reality, the blood of Jesus.

In most protestant churches, I suppose that would mean the Welch's grape juice would metamorphose into the blood of Christ. I'm not sure we think of it that way. The wafer and beverage are just symbols. The grape juice is for "safety first." We cannot risk serving real wine to those struggling with alcohol.

Luther had proposed "consubstantiation." The difference was that the sacramental elements became vehicles of the "Real Presence of Christ" in, with, and under the bread and wine, and not the real thing in itself. What do you think? Can you tell the difference? (Isn't theology great? See what you've been missing all these years?)

I had no idea how all of these theological and philosophical concepts could provide hope for those who despair, healing for those who hurt, love for the lonely, reconciliation for the estranged, courage for the dispossessed, faith for the desperate. But I learned a lot of stuff, and now it was time to put it to the test.

When I arrived in California, my ordination papers had not been transferred. My new District Superintendent attempted to call the Oklahoma Bishop to expedite the papers. The long distance operator (in those days), said that the Bishop was out in the pasture with his cattle. My new D.S. said to tell them to look for the "bull with the hat on!" Maybe I should have bought the Bishop a hat, after all!

CHAPTER 7

CORNUCOPIA

THEOS

"What is faith? It is the confident assurance that
something we want is going to happen. It is the
certainty that what we hope for is waiting for us,
even though we cannot see it up ahead."

(Hebrews 11:1-2) TLB

I still recall the astonishing beauty of the Monterey Peninsula as
I overlooked the bay from Highway One for the first time. The
bay was an elliptical blue-green jewel, framed by a glistening crescent
shoreline.

It took my breath away. The sparkling sands, scintillating fog,
rustic houses, narrow surface roads, brilliant ice plant, rhododendron,
bougainvillea, cypress trees, eucalyptus, madrone, blue bay, white
beaches, white caps, rocky coast lines, were a feast for the senses, a
riot of color.

The coastal drive opened up my nostrils, and the sweet, fresh air filled my lungs. "Lover's Point" in Pacific Grove was never crowded, and the quaint, appealing architecture of the houses overlooking the bay made me pull over by the side of the road and just take it all in.

Most houses on the Peninsula were hidden in small lanes and behind refulgent shrubs. *"How sweet, how fresh, this vernal day; how musical the air. Nature was never seen so gay, were but my Sylvia near. Hush, wanton, wanton birds, your amorous songs arouse my tender breast."* The Seminary Singers sang that song at S. M.U., but I never understood it before. *"Retire, sweet whistling winds, retire."*

Strolling down lanes in Carmel-By-The-Sea was exaltation for the culturally starved soul. The Bach Festival, the Monterey Jazz Festival, the "Concours de Elegance," the Rancho Seco auto races, the art studios with live artists at work, coffee houses, theatre offerings (California's First Theatre), Asilomar, lectures, the constant servings of head stuff and heart stuff was quite stimulating. Deep sea fishing was exhilarating, and I was in very deep cultural seas.

This was in 1955, before the freeway "can of worms," as opponents called it, was built. One could stroll out to the "Crosby Clambake" on Pebble Beach, and walk right up to Bing Crosby, Ben Hogan, Phil Harris, Burt Lancaster (of Elmer Gantry fame), or Jack Lemmon, right up close and personal. There were no roped off areas, no security, no problems. One could take their pictures on the first tee, or later in the course of play. Even the ultra-exclusive Cypress Point course was part of the tour. It was heady.

Buckminster Fuller gave lectures at Monterey Peninsula College, and seemed to know everything. Another one of those guys. I took classes in oils and pastels at the Art School, and astonished myself with my primitive talent. I even sold one to an admirer.

I was thriving in a horn of plenty. It was all a matter of "shock and awe" for the little lad from Oklahoma. Jesus had spoken of the "Life Abundant," and this looked like it was as near heaven on earth as anything I could have ever imagined. I knew I had made the right decision.

My little flocks in Oklahoma had been farmers and ranchers

and small town pilgrims. My new constituents were professors and lawyers and doctors and old money and middle to upper class pilgrims. The folk ranged from affluent to financially struggling. My best friends and supporters owned a dry cleaning shop. This family was the light of my world.

One of the men who helped us kick-start the enterprise was a banker, who became a close friend. He was prospering, and soon to become very rich, thanks to the growth of the branches and sound investments. He had his own closet mode of suffering, (no, he was not gay), but while helping to create the money for us to build, he loved to usher on Sunday mornings. He was a sound, loving, encouraging partner, who put our new church on solid ground.

Another delightful interlude came in the form of a "Great Books" club, to which I was invited. We spent Tuesday evenings with our host, the associate editor of the Monterey Peninsula Herald. He was a brilliant man, who surfed Sophocles and others with us to stretch the minds of doctors and lawyers and merchants and me.

After 19 years of education, my preaching was a struggle between Biblical exposition and current affairs and theological quandaries. It wasn't very good, but patient and forgiving people still came to church. Preparing sermons was total agony, and always put off until the last minute. I had a good sense of humor around town and in civic meetings, but took myself way too seriously in the pulpit.

One evening we were invited to a small dinner party atop the hill, "Monte Vista," in Monterey. We looked out at the semicircle of night lights as they drew a half moon around Monterey Bay. A retired pastor from Canada was one of the guests. In one of my naively ambitious moments I asked him, "How do you break into a town like this?" He gently and wisely replied, "Just by quietly going about your business."

We did have many idyllic moments. There was the annual "Live Nativity Scene," with young military men and women donning the traditional Christmas apparel, and standing out in the cold for hours in the evening, while my recorded narration and taped music wafted through the air. There were ski trips to the mountains for young people, and endless potluck dinners and celebrations.

I was working my way into the "in group" of powerbrokers among my colleagues. One evening my wife and I were invited to a small dinner in Carmel. The Bishop and his wife, the pastor of the Church of the Wayfarer with his wife, Dick and Jane (first wife). Things were good.

One of the strangest episodes included the son of our Bishop who was a Red Cross worker at Fort Ord. I don't remember how we met, but we became close friends, and he would come over each Sunday night for a glass of wine and companionship.

Of course, winebibbing was strictly taboo in the Methodist Church at that time, and my good Bishop, not knowing, could never understand our friendship. The son was an "unbeliever," but a "seeker" of the truth of the first order. We had a "communion service" of our very own.

My Red Cross friend and I always followed Ben Franklin's advice: "drink not to elevation." He even came to church a few times, a thing which he had not done since heaven knows when. It's not easy to be a "PK" (preacher's kid). I know full well how they can develop allergies to "religion." They see the altar from inside the veil. It's kind of like the Wizard of Oz when Dorothy got behind the screen.

We were planted in the midst of a military mega-mix. There was Fort Ord, the U.S. Naval Postgraduate School, the Army Language School, and other such institutions all around us. I went to the chaplains of each of these institutions and asked for, and was granted, the names of the Methodists among their personnel. Then I took the posture of a "Fuller Brush Man," and went door to door, inviting these young families to attend our church. Many did, and our attendance shot straight up.

Army and Navy personnel bring army and navy wives. It seemed as though all these cheerleaders had grown up and married their dream kings. Many were very happily married. A few were most unhappy and most unfulfilled. Some pastoral calls were very scary.

I recall being greeted at the door by a real naval beauty. I was ushered into her house warmly. Attempting to neutralize the ions, I sat down on her piano bench and began to demonstrate my pianoforte. She sidled up to the bench on her knees, shoulders now bare, and I was suddenly looking down into the valley of Eden. Her eyes said, "all is yours." It was treat or retreat. I fled.

At age 26 I had my own "Cannery Row" going. It was a helluva lot more interesting than John Steinbeck's, and a lot more disastrous inside me, and I began to think that perhaps I'd better get out of the ministry before I created too big a diversion for the socially elite on the Peninsula.

Even though I had read and underlined "The Divine Imperative" by Emil Brunner, I was not prepared for this kind of "Emotional Imperative"! I guess in Seminary I had had too much "Word," and now I was having too much "Flesh." There's a fine balance in there somewhere, but I had yet to manage the equilibrium. I was experiencing a kaleidoscope of thoughts, feelings, ambitions, doubts, and distractions. I had a "hole in my bucket."

I began to wonder what kind of man I would be if I hadn't grown up in the "Bible Belt." I revisited my early entry into the "profession" of the minister, and my seemingly irrelevant theologies. I was very curious about the lives of the business and professional friends who seemed to have a wider scope of living and understanding than I.

My concerns extended to the body of The Methodist Church at large. (This was before it merged with the Evangelical United Brethren Church and became The United Methodist Church.) The so-called "Social Gospel" had won the balance between Social Justice and Personal Holiness. It is of little wonder that the membership in "main stream" denominations plunged into a severe decline in the next several decades.

Most Methodist lay people didn't feel they came to church to hear how to think or vote on the endless line of social issues. They wanted a few "crumbs under the table" about how to grow spiritually into the love of Christ, and how to understand themselves as pilgrims on a holy journey. Instead, for the most part, they heard about the journeyman on the road of social rights. Food for the soul was hard to find.

"Church Wisdom" on the subject of social issues is generally a cultural and geographical phenomenon. The wisdom of the

Conferences in the South and Southeast is quite contrary to the wisdom of the West and the Northeast. The clashes of politics and religion are ongoing.

Annual Conference sessions became battlegrounds for "Righteousness by Resolution." Preaching became "prophetic" if you took on cultural and social and political issues, and the spiritual health of pastor and people took second place. Pronouncements from the General Conference became a matter of division for folks on the local level. Liberal bishops making proclamations were incendiary as far as the person in the pew was concerned.

One of my great prophetic moments came when I tackled the flaming Methodist banner of total abstinence from alcohol. Along came "Temperance Sunday," in the fall of each year. All Methodists were given a pledge card, and the opportunity and encouragement to commit to total abstinence from all alcoholic beverages. "Demon rum."

In a blaze of prophetic fury, I preached a two-part sermon series entitled "The Right to Drink." The first sermon traced the concept of abstinence into the church (born of Wesley's time, in a culture of drunkenness, abuse and dissipation in a Dickensonian England). The concept was about 150 years old at the time I took it on. The second sermon promised to reveal my own ideas on the subject.

The church was packed on the second Sunday. One of my pagan friends planted a bottle of vodka in the pulpit, so I held it up before I began to speak and assured my flock that it would be "properly disposed of."

I strove boldly forward with my theme that one could drink responsibly or irresponsibly, just as one could abstain responsibly or irresponsibly. The lifting of the long nose by Methodists who didn't drink made few friends of non-believers, and added a rather smug air of righteousness and exclusiveness to the situation. Most good Methodists were and are social drinkers anyway, and I am unaware of any sermon that changed any mind on the subject.

Alcohol has ruined lives, no doubt. Romance has ruined lives, sex has ruined lives, food has ruined lives, television and music have ruined lives, automobiles have ruined lives, boats have ruined lives, prescription drugs, and ad infinitum. As St. Paul said, "whether you drink or whether you eat, do so for the glory of God." "Temperance" is good. Legalism is not. Jesus is said to have turned water into wine at a wedding. We don't know whether it was white or red. But it is reported in the Bible to have been the best of the evening's celebration. Oh, for just a sip of that Jesus wine!

I sent copies of my salutary sermons to several of my colleagues. Before long, I got a letter from the Bishop on Christmas Eve. "Merry Christmas!" He said that he had heard that I was preaching "contrary to the Discipline of the Church," and wanted to know more about it. I sent him copies of the two sermons, and never heard back.

When I left the ministry, the Bishop called me to express his disappointment. "You are the only pastor who touched my son," he said. Little did he know what I used to "touch him," and I never said "a mumblin' word." Most bishops are too busy "bishoping" to be pastor to the pastors, which should be their primary function. They deal with the "larger issues" of church and society.

We kept Route 66 hot between California and Oklahoma City. Every summer included a trip to my "holy land" of Holdenville, to visit family and friends. There was no air conditioning in our cars, so we looked for motels with swimming pools all along the way. Barstow, Needles, Albuquerque, and Amarillo all offered cheap overnighters and quick early morning getaways. My parents and brother's family restored my soul.

The great guru Eric Berne was shining in Carmel with his "What Do You Say After You Say Hello" Transactional Analysis breakthrough, and I saw him occasionally at the coffee shop, but I dared not approach him. I would encounter his thought years later in Sacramento, in the hands of rather competent people.

Tod was the name of another significant player. He was a retired Presbyterian minister. Actually, he wasn't retired at all. He was dying of cancer while he was only in his fifties, and so he had to quit and stay at home. His beautiful and talented wife sold real estate to keep their ship afloat, and she located and sold us our first parsonage on Monterey Circle.

Tod volunteered to be our choir director. A Methodist choir led by a Presbyterian pastor who was dying of cancer, and fortunately for our young church, it took him a couple of years or more to die.

He was very handsome, a sweet spirit, an extremely intelligent fellow with an impeccable taste for good choir music and could bring out the very best of the two dozen that responded to his inspiration and skill. Tod gave me his pulpit robe. I'd never bothered to get one, and really couldn't afford to buy one. Tod was looking straight into his abyss, and moved bravely (serenely) forward, day-by-day.

So here was Tod, listening to me struggle with my strange mixture of newly acquired theology, articles from Newsweek and Time, stories from the Reader's Digest, a hot article from "The Christian Century" by some prominent theology prof, and, oh yes, a scripture lesson. I was strung out every Saturday night, because I had always waited until then to finalize my sermon.

About midnight I would usually say OK, enough is enough, and stroll over to the new Hofbrau on the hill next door to the church. The owners were friends who would pour me a beer in a big plastic cup and call it a milkshake and hand it to me as my reward for getting through another trial by fire at my church office. That's because we (the church) didn't raise a stink when a bar moved into our neighborhood, and way too close for zoning purposes.

I can't even imagine the patience and understanding that it took for Tod to endure my sermons, to cope with his ever-increasing discomfort and illness, to ignore his pain during choir practices each week, and to appear perfectly well and poised on Sunday mornings. He was a walking sermon, and taught me a lot more than any prof or colleague I had known. Yes, he died, and I had the honor of speaking at his funeral. His widow was gracious and serene, and moved on with her life.

It still seemed very clear to me that the love of Jesus had something to say about this kind of existential moment, and that there was truth waiting to be revealed to me, and to everyone I knew, but that it could never be put into words or sermons or songs or theologies or poetry or art or any kind of container. But it was still there, mystifying me.

My belief system had been diluted, and I had deepening questions about the doctrine of the Trinity, the doctrine of the Virgin Birth, the doctrine of Catholic (Universal) Church, the Apostles' Creed, and all the other postulations that those wiseacres in the fourth century at Nicea had reached by compromise after 300 years of confusion and complexities and competition since the coming and going of Jesus. What the church fathers did was to invent a religion out of the straw fragmentary writings owned by geographical gurus.

The Apostles did not write the "Apostles' Creed", nor did they ever recite it.

"Church Fathers," not mothers, wrote the book of creeds and rituals. Women, though they had been the primary "support group" for Jesus in his travels (according to the Gospels), had no voice or influence. St. Paul had seen to that. Thanks to his foolishness, women were subjugated, in terms of input, output, or any other put. They were just supposed to "put out," and have male babies who would grow up and tell them how to behave and what to believe. *"Res ipsa loquiter."* The thing speaks for itself.

After all, Mary of Magadala was the first person to whom the risen Christ showed himself. She was the one who ran to report the resurrection to the unbelieving disciples, who were later elevated to the rank of "Apostle."

The great overlay of doctrine and theology and ritual and tradition became all too sterile, and I decided I could no longer hide behind the "Reverend" crap and the ordained vs. the non-ordained. I was just a guy, and wanted only to be a guy with all my heart. My hormones and homilies and hopes had degenerated to become dry bones. I felt like a crepe myrtle in winter, just a bare bunch of brittle branches connected to an austere trunk.

I remembered the saying of a then famous theology prof: "The church is like Noah's Ark; if it were not for the storm outside, you couldn't stand the smell inside." For most people, inside and out, the perception of the Bible was that of George Bernard Shaw's character John Tarleton in "Misalliance:" "The Bible, oh, I read it once. Not bad!"

But there are faithful people who redeem us all. Like the Jewish limousine driver I once hailed down in New York City, trying to get over to New Jersey. We had quite a bit of time on our hands en route, and he did quite a bit of talking.

He had been a prisoner in Auschwitz during WWII, and he showed me the numbers on his arm. He said that after the war a friend had used those numbers to bet on some kind of lottery, and he won big time. "That's good," he said, "One man's misfortune is another man's fortune." Now that was great theology!

Martin Buber had written about going from the "I" to the "Thou" and avoiding the "It." I think my chauffeur had a real handle on this. "Life is a bitter/sweet waltz."

Somerset Maugham wrote "Of Human Bondage," and how stupid the doctor was to be obsessed with an ignorant waitress, and how many hundreds of pages the pain went on and how disgusted I was with the whole unbelievable idea, never realizing my own bondage and obsessions and compulsions and barreling through it all and managing to build a church and attract a flock and leave a going concern.

Well, I had truly felt the call of God to go into the ministry. Now I truly felt it was God's will for me to move on, to get out, to see the world from a different perspective altogether. After all, Martin Luther had broken all of his vows of chastity, poverty, and obedience. Why shouldn't I? Luther was a "lost sheep," as far as his (Roman Catholic) church was concerned. He not only never came back, he threw stones at his "adulteress" church, and had a theological ball. Then he married a nun, had drunken dinners with friends and vulgar conversations about God and the church, and lived the abundant life. Why couldn't I?

CHAPTER 8

THE FAR COUNTRY

CHAOS

"The younger son said to his father, 'Father, I
want right now what's coming to me.' It wasn't
long before the younger son packed his bags and
left for a distant country."

Luke 15:11-13 (TLB)

I got what I wanted out of the ministry. I got out! Now I was on
my way to the top. I was no longer tied down to a petty
bunch of prigs who would take two or three years to consider
increasing my salary by $25.00 per month. Do you think I was
angry?

Having lived in a "parsonage" for five years, we had no home
of our own. My good banker friend offered me a job, but I
could not see working in an enclosed environment and staying in
the same community. I needed to "get out of town."

One of my church members was a fine looking, charismatic

young man who was an assistant manager with MONY, Mutual of New York. In one or two conversations he "converted" me from pastor to peddler.

The agency was centered in San Jose, and the manager convinced me that I should break all ties with Monterey, move to San Jose, where I knew no one, and launch out into the deep and learn that I could survive anywhere. It was scary, but I took him up on it. He proved to be right.

We found a modest new house in San Jose, and the adventure began. The first shock came when my trainer handed me a rate book. It looked the size of a New Testament. All it contained was columns of figures. My weakest link in education was math. Suddenly I was thrust into the world of numbers and estimates and formulas.

It was "rate book shock." I discovered the number ten, and how to divide and multiply and estimate and discern mortality tables and life insurance premiums. With a very few simple explanations of term life, whole life, and endowment policies, I stepped out into the great unknown world of "prospecting."

"Let this line represent your life line," was the line I was to use. I "killed" people off one at a time, and sold a lot of life insurance. I came very close to being a "million dollar" producer my first year.

I hated "prospecting." The idea of meeting all new people with an eye fixed on how soon I could get into their living rooms to talk about insurance was totally strange and repulsive to me. I lived off Pepto Bismol.

The manager chose me "Man of the Year" at the end of my first year in the agency. Before long the Assistant Sales Manager moved on to another company, and the position was open. I maneuvered my way into the job, and carried on for two more years.

I had big dreams, big aspirations, and big cars. I bought a "Starfire" Oldsmobile, a Starfish sailboat, and I was a star salesman! We bought a new house, had great neighbors, went to church (to worship and to meet new prospects), and had the "perfect" life.

After all, if Robert Pirsig could find the "Zen" in motorcycle maintenance, surely I could find the eye of the Buddha in selling life insurance. I had read "Psycho Cybernetics," and knew all I had to do was to picture myself over the top, and there I would be.

If you're a good salesman, you get sent to a lot of conventions. So I got my first taste of airports, taxis, hotels, bars, and late dinners. As some famous preacher once said, "He was not free, he was just unzipped!"

Pillow came to see me in San Jose. Now that I was free from the chains of the clergy, she assumed I was available and ready to go all the way. She said she had talked it over with her husband, and he had given us permission to play in the Garden of Eden to our hearts delight. I was petrified. I saw her husband a few weeks later, and he said to me, "You're a lucky man, Richard. You're the one she has chosen!" I assured him I had no intention of going the distance. That was the last I saw of Pillow for over two decades.

One of the most inspirational speakers I have ever heard was Charlie "Tremendous!" Jones. He would waltz around the conference floor telling riveting stories of success and failure and recovery. Everything for Charlie was "Tremendous!" If you were planning your days correctly and executing the sale, that was Tremendous! If you were dying of cancer, that was Tremendous! If you were going through bankruptcy or divorce, that was Tremendous! Because every door shutting was a new door opening, and that was, indeed, Tremendous! If your life wasn't Tremendous, then you were simply not aware of life.

Then we listened to another guru on "living death:" that is to say, how to sell disability insurance. Most people could afford to die, but they couldn't afford to live and not have or not be able to make an income. He was good. But I sold very few "disability income" policies.

It was during this test of endurance that I was inspired to take up the classical and folk guitar. Again, music soothed my soul, and I found great comfort in strumming classical tunes, singing folk songs and even inventing a few.

While I had been in Monterey, I had come across a group

counseling process called "Prayer Therapy." We took a series of personality tests, which "indicated" our personality types, and how we would handle the "four basic emotions: fear, rage, love, and wonder." It was interesting, and helpful at that stage. So in San Jose I began a new group of five couples that met in our home once a week. There were two architects, a real estate tycoon, et al, with spouses. I was very good at it. Most of us ended up in divorce.

I don't remember how or why, but I took up practicing hypnotism at cocktail parties. I was pretty good at it. It was "fun," but as a friend of mine used to say, "all trouble starts out as fun." Nothing came of it, but I quit risking the game on innocent victims.

After four years with MONY, I had an offer I couldn't refuse from Ohio National Life Insurance Company to open a branch in San Jose. The mission was to build an agency from scratch, and the upfront funding was generous. It was time to move out and move on.

The first year was productive, and we ended up with five full time agents. At the national gathering of General Agents (managers) in Cincinnati, I gave a little speech, which was well received, and I received an offer to become National Director of Training and move to Cincinnati. I could have leapfrogged into the home office.

I pondered the move for a few weeks, and then declined. I didn't want to live in Ohio and leave my beautiful California. About six months later all of my agents developed a symptom called "lack of production," and I resigned from Ohio National. It was a sour end to a bright beginning.

During those earlier halcyon days, Rob van der Toorren and I produced a play in San Jose at the Unitarian Church called "Murder in the Cathedral," the story of the martyrdom of the Archbishop of Canterbury. Rob also taught me how to sail my little "El Toro" on the placid waters of Lake Vasona near Saratoga. It was there I learned about the boom and the luff and the jibe and the tack. Those were euphoric moments.

During these uncertain business days of ups and downs, my first wife and I sought counseling to analyze what had gone wrong with our marriage. Through our friends in the church we found a psychiatrist who was building a practice, and we enrolled in weekly sessions of examination and sharing with other couples. This one was for real.

It proved to be a serious mistake, as the "good doctor" had his own agenda for his patients, and divorce became the order of the day, and the end result of most of his "expertise." Every time he goofed up, he said, "I think this will make me a better psychiatrist!" It was all about him, not an uncommon trait of the average shrink. He refunded all of the money we had advanced him over a two-year period, but profound and irreparable damage had been done to our marriage. He later lost his license to practice.

After the Ohio National debacle, I received a very timely phone call from a recruiter who represented the Security Life of Denver, and I accepted a position as "Regional Manager."

We moved to Sacramento, and I began to travel my territory, from Redding to Fresno and Reno to Davis. I was "on the road again," well funded, and filled with new hope for a promising career.

In essence I was a "pirate," attempting to recruit successful agents from other insurance companies into our enterprise. So my days were filled with calling and engaging in appointments with salespeople from all walks of the insurance industry. It was interesting and informative, and once again I began to gather a small contingent of salesmen into the company.

The move to Sacramento had been somewhat of a culture shock. I hated the thought of leaving the Bay Area, the zone of all the cultural "action." It was to prove to be a huge blessing in disguise, although that wasn't revealed until much later.

After about a year on the road, my first marriage of fourteen years collapsed. We had drifted too far apart, and there seemed to be no return. Sadness filled my soul. "There ain't no good guys, there ain't no bad guys, there's just you and me and we just disagree," as the song goes.

The toughest part was taking a small trip with each son, one at a time, to the nearby "A&W" root beer stand. While sharing a treat with them I tried to explain the unexplainable, why their parents were splitting up. Shock, disbelief, sadness was their response, and I could only hope that some day they would see the light of day and end up feeling loved by their Mom and Dad fully and completely.

I thought things were going very well with Security Life. I had been with them for five years, the last of which I had led the way in recruitment. I was asked to give a little talk on my success at the annual gathering of regional sales managers. A month later I was invited to San Francisco for what I thought would be a raise and a promotion. I was greeted by my boss at the San Francisco International Airport, who informed me that I no longer had a job. Another surprise ending, like the sudden execution by the Oklahoma District Superintendent.

Ouch! This really took the wind out of my sails. I took the long drive home with no apparent prospects for the future. By this time I was living in a crummy apartment in "lower Sacramento," and had no financial reserves.

In all of my apparent successes in the life insurance industry, I was always trembling on the brink. I tried a brief fling with Firemen's Fund, which was starting up a new life insurance division, but my spirit and mind were depleted. I was ready to add to Law's "Varieties of Religious Experience," but I couldn't find a category that hadn't been taken, except despair.

One of my friends had said that he had been inoculated: that is, he had just enough religion to be immune to it! That's about where I was. Now my holy sites were in bars, bedrooms, and smelly rooms for rent. I was a falling star. The lights went out. The party was over.

I remembered looking into the fireplace at my friend Carlton Whitehead's house many years ago in Monterey, and saying that I felt I was being consumed just as one of the logs. I was ready for a stroll in the wilderness, and a wrestling match with one of Jacob's dark angels.

CHAPTER 9

THE ELEGANT BARN

BATHOS

> "No doubt about it! God is good. But as for me, I came so close to the edge of the cliff. My feet were slipping and I was almost gone."
>
> Psalm 73:2 (TLB)

THE DESCENT

Now with two degrees in theology, a record of church building, and a California license to sell life insurance, what should I do next? I was 40 years old, with no car, and no clear direction in front of me. I drifted from one employment agency to another, but no opportunities appealed to me.

I didn't want to go on with my life insurance "career." I could have moved to Ohio or some other Eastern or Southern state, presented my credentials, and carried on. But I couldn't bring myself to leave Northern California. Maybe Abe Lincoln felt like this when he kept on losing elections, and got into a funk. Winston Churchill had his "Black Dog" of a depression, which would assault him from time to time. Was Picasso's "Blue Period" all about this?

It is reported that one of the 18th century mystics, Emanuel Swedenborg, had his moments of despondency. He endured nightmares, and his "gross thoughts" were represented to him in a dream as heaps of rags. His impurities were perceived as vermin, which had to be picked out. "Bizarre schemes, hideous images, lustful urges, grosser impulses . . ." tore through his mind as he attempted to sort out and eliminate the negative from his consciousness. These struggles, like St. Paul's, proved to be the road to inner freedom.

A very successful pastor of a large church in San Jose (different denomination) had previously been referred to me to inquire about a career in life insurance. He was a handsome man with a lot of charisma. He managed to squeeze into our conversation that "making out" with beautiful women had always been easy for him. Now instead of another woman, he was looking for another career. He would have made a damn fine insurance salesman, but he went on with his "profession." Too many perks, I guess. He, too, was wrestling with the angels.

I know of an esteemed clerical colleague of mine, at the "top of the pile," who once went through a period contemplating suicide. Dark thoughts invade all of us from time to time. The gravity of negativity can lay hands on any of us.

At this point, and in this view, I was in pretty good company, but I didn't look at it that way at the time. Now I was learning all about existentialism. For a few months I was one step away from being homeless. I lived in "rooms" for rent, and walked the streets of Sacramento, job-hunting, living on cans of salmon and pinto beans. As the old king said, "There's no good sauce like hunger!"

I felt like one of those Kafkan cockroaches, and it looked very much like I was stuck in an inescapable labyrinth of unhappiness. As the "Villagers" sang: "It's fun to stay at the YMCA."

One of my classy lady friends said that it looked like I had decided to become an "indigent"! Well, I had, for the time being. "Stop the world," I just wanted to get off! Now things were much more visceral than spiritual. In this dark period I was emotionally, mentally and spiritually depleted.

"The Elegant Barn" was a hippie, cook your own steakhouse, with punk live entertainment. The acrid odor of marijuana wafted through the dingy, dark, drab, reclaimed barn-wood walls. I was through with life insurance for good, and had become a habitué of this quaint little restaurant. *All the lonely people, where do they all come from?*"

Thus it was that I was offered a job. The life of a bartender is not all drinks and drunks. In a way, a bartender can be a pastor, just as anyone else who serves the public. People turn to firemen, plumbers, carpet cleaners, hair stylists, and most anyone in times of crisis. I know my wife, a cosmetologist, has been a pastor to many, many people over the years, listening, counseling, and sharing very good information regarding health, marriage, divorce, and life and death situations.

The TV series "Cheers" shows that people like to go "where everybody knows your name." I think when I served drinks and nibbles some evenings it had the same bonding impact on my new "flock." It would be a place where Jesus would be quite at home, "eating and drinking with sinners". Church people tend to forget that God is quite as much at work in the cesspools of life as ever in the "together" folk and the "nice" places. Most bars are not "cesspools," but this one came close.

John Wesley wrote in his Journal dated May 25, 1764: "I preached . . . . to a very elegant congregation. But I expect little good will be done here. For we begin at the wrong end. Religion must not go 'from the greatest to the least,' or the power would 'appear to be of men.'" If God starts at the bottom, I was there.

Real food and wine is what the disciples shared with Jesus. If the first Disciples ever came on the scene of the typical Christian church with its wine (or grape juice) and wafers, I think they would be astonished. They would wonder, "Where's the Love Feast?"

The Disciples did not become winos (though some, St Paul suggests, drank to excess.) They simply knew how to celebrate the love of their Master. What we call "Mass" or "Communion" is a far cry from the Last Supper. The Scottish Rite has it right. One Maundy Thursday evening after I spoke to them they served wine and roast beef sandwiches. Now that's a love feast.

I decided to supplement my pauper's wages by making candles. Gathering empty aluminum cans (scrounging, that is), I learned from the craft shop to use wicks and wax to shape small candles that fit inside "hippie" candleholders. A friend had passed through the Elegant Barn and introduced me to his craft with coffee cans and an acetylene torch.

So my evening hours were spent over the small stove in my cheap apartment, producing candles for the restaurant. It was a desperate measure, but it gave me money for food and shelter and weird, funky clothes, appropriate to my new station in life.

I purchased an old motorcycle. It was my only means of transportation. I reread Pirsig's "Zen and the Art of Motorcycle Maintenance," but it didn't remind me to turn on the gas switch of my primitive machine before I started trying to pump the pedal to start my engine.

I had learned in seminary that in every crucifixion there was a latent resurrection, but when you're "on the cross" it's hard to remember that kind of thing. Maybe that's why Jesus cried out "My God, why have you forsaken me?"

I was dead broke. If things come in threes, I was in the third degree. I had gone through a divorce, lost my job, and now my oldest son was "losing his mind." The tragedy of my son Mark was the lowest point in my life. He and four other boys (age 19ish) sat down on the living room floor of my apartment one New Year's Eve. They took something (LSD?), and Mark took leave of his senses. The other four young men got up the next day to lead "normal" lives. Mark was never to return. He became an acute case of "paranoid-schizophrenic."

From that point on, Mark was to endure psychological mismanagement from several sources. He was in and out of jails, hospitals, emergency rooms, mental wards, and in the hands of wrong doctors and counselors. Of course, this was in the 70's, and few professionals knew how to diagnose or treat the many variations of mental illness.

Mark was the unfortunate recipient of wrong medications, wrong handling, wrong everything. He ended up in Atascadero, a prison for the criminally insane! He had done no criminal act, nor hurt anyone. He was simply hard to control, and would not voluntarily take his medications. A friend of mine said that Mark took drugs once, and the State of California drugged him every day after that.

The problem in the "hospital" in Atascadero was that the prison "counselors" unwittingly prescribed chemicals that actually intensified the paranoia rather than mitigated the condition. They would let him out of prison from time to time, but give him a different form of medication to take "on the streets" that would actually drive him nuts, and then he would have to return to the prison. Picked up by cops, thrown in jail, back to Atascadero. It was a vicious cycle.

I had been informed by one of the counselors that I should stay out of Mark's problem. She said that I was providing a counterproductive "cushion" for him, and Mark wouldn't wise up to the fact that he had to take his medications on his own. She said public agencies would withdraw their assistance if they knew they could turn him back over to his family, and "people get sick at home." That's where it started, after all.

The absolute nadir of my experience happened one hot summer day. Mark unexpectedly showed up at our house in a taxi. He came in, sweaty and disheveled, wearing cowboy boots up to his knees. His feet and legs were full of blisters the size of half-dollars. Remembering the advice of the counselor, I asked Mark to get in my car. I said we would go for a ride.

We did. I took him miles away from our house to the streets in mid-town Sacramento. It was evening. I said, "Mark, get out of the car." He did, and I drove away! I cried all the way home, and for days to come. (He was picked up that evening, and was back in the hands of caregivers, but I didn't know that at the time.) Mark was later to say, "Dad, you made me alligator bait!" My son Mark is a master of metaphors. Mixed, that is. For example:

> "I don't like prison. If I go to prison, I hope it's Soledad.
> The bars have a sense of humor in Soledad."
>
> "We can't make up our mind, Mark; we don't know what to
> call it, "*Mutiny on the Bounty,*" or what was it? I didn't
> do nothing but blow my own belly button. I can't get
> off the trampoline very well. I have too much fun."
>
> "Am I supposed to be in high school for the rest of my life?
> From what I can tell, I'm a burnt out U-2 spy plane. I
> might as well be a U.S. postage stamp. Send me to the
> back-to-the-woods school. I'll be in the woods
> predominantly, prehistorically. Riding pterodactyls."

Mark summarized his thoughts: "I need to have enough patience to wait on myself and it will descend and I will be one again. I'm preludes."

There were times when I wished that Mark had died, instead of just becoming "an empty shell." I began to feel like the story of Dorian Gray, rather handsome on the outside, but ugly as sin on the inside. I was so filled with fear and guilt and shame. I suspected it was I who had caused all of Mark's suffering, rather than a "chemical imbalance" or other theories on the phenomenon. Maybe God was punishing me for having left my calling.

After about a ten-year malaise for Mark, he began to mellow. It was years and years of living hell, but Mark chose to survive. Mark, the real Mark, my son, began to re-emerge. The "shell" was now occupied with a living soul, and we could connect and bond and love each other.

When I think of all that Mark had to endure, I marvel at his success. He may not have had a life of "production" by worldly standards, but he has raised the bar for others who are suffering. I am grateful for his stamina and perseverance. Now he is a joy to talk to, and his eyes are filled with love. He has forgiven so much, and moved on. We have lunch once a month, and have nutty conversations. (But then I have nutty conversations with everyone, every day.)

Meanwhile, I was grudgingly known by the "cocktail waitresses" in the Elegant Barn as a "slow pour." They would step up to me, having taken the orders from a table of eight, and rattle off the orders. Now a good mixologist would know the system, and arrange the appropriate glasses in front of him in the right order as a reminder. But when she gave me her order of eight, I would simply say, "Now which two drinks would you like first?"

Carole King was singin' my song: "I felt the earth move, under my skin . . . I felt the sky come a tumbalin' down, a tumbalin' down, a tumbalin' down . . . . all over, all over." I felt it was just about all over, too. It reminded me of Paul Tillich's super book, "The Shaking of the Foundations," in which everybody's world, and every culture, sooner or later, collapses.

Had I finally run smack into what Kierkegaard called "The Sickness Unto Death"?

I guess I was living out "Pilgrim's Regress," and had taken another dip into John Bunyan's "slough of despond."

In that superb term paper back in theology school I had drawn a simile of life in the un-awakened state as a life lived in a brick house, versus the spiritually awakened state as a life lived in a glass house. In the brick house you would look at your surroundings and see only what was in front of you. In the glass house you always see beyond the walls, out there. You are aware that you always live in two different worlds, the seen and the unseen.

I had crawled back into the brick house at this stage of the game. My world was quite opaque, and I couldn't see through anything. St. Paul said we all "see through a glass darkly," but mine was all bricks.

For a while I shared Mark's "madness." I tried marijuana, and discovered my own paranoia. Riding my motorcycle stoned one day, I ended up in some grocery store, about 30 miles away from my dingy hovel. Strolling up and down the aisles, I was seized by fear, and I was sure that every person in the store was out to hurt me, or worse. I fled the store, mounted my motorcycle, and strained with all my might to stay alert and alive, fighting blurred vision, as I drove through Sacramento searching for my apartment.

Now I knew were Mark was, and how he got there. He just couldn't make it back. I vowed that it was the end of my experiment. I don't know how I survived that ride, except that my guardian angel was doing overtime. My "self-esteem" had evaporated, and I was clinging to life by my fingernails.

I did learn from Mark that one cannot afford to "go down" when you're attempting to help someone else. You can be of little help if you, too, "crash and burn" in an effort to lift someone else back up.

Meanwhile, back at the bar, I listened to a hundred stories. The chef was a guy named Jack who had once been a professional radio announcer in Chicago. He, too, had come a long way down the ladder. He was a brilliant man, but had lost hold of his grip on life, so he made a good soul mate for me. Our family had him in our home often on Thanksgiving Days and other holidays for the next few years after my recovery.

The owners of the "Barn" were all "financially advantaged" but they managed to have problems of their own. We were all "pilgrims," swimming upstream, spitting against the wind. For me, as Queen Elizabeth once said, it was an "Anis Horribilis!" But it wasn't all bad.

Among my "clients" were spouse swappers, "swingers," "key club" players, high-rollers, lowlifes, and hippies. The swappers were not flakes. They were very successful business and professional people in their own right. They just needed to do something in the evening besides play bridge.

As Frank Sinatra sang, "It was a very good year." I had read Jacob Bronowski's "Ascent of Man," but I'm not sure I was sharing in the Ascension. Someone said that all that prostitutes talk about is God, and all that priests talk about is sex. I wasn't serving either clientele, but the conversations roamed the range of the human condition. I learned the difference between "screamers" and "moaners" and others who "can't get no satisfaction." Life just seemed to be one big wet dream.

One of the swappers told me that she had found a far better lover than her husband, and she was going to make a serious change, and switch over to the new man. And she did. Now I don't know if the new lover made a better husband, or how that all came out. They were charter members of the "5 H Club:" Happy, Healthy, Hungry, Horny, and Hopeful."

They were all in search of what Abigail Adams called, the "Happy shock!"

The primary function of a bartender is not to pour drinks, but to listen. Like my father would say, "Let's have a talk, Richard." Then we would sit down and I would listen for hours. I was his teenage therapist in those days, without either one of us knowing it. Of course, I had no idea what was going on, but I did learn. I learned how to listen.

What is it about a bartender that stimulates empathy and interest from the opposite sex? I was never more broke, and it was never easier to have company. Offers to the right of me, offers to the left of me, offers in front of me, "volleyed and thundered!" Of course, I accepted on occasion. Were these fine ladies not "angels of God's mercy" in my desperado days? I was dead broke, but in the sense of companionship, I had "struck gold!" These female entities tickled my fancy, and I theirs, and it was all "ring around the rosy." One exceptional beauty took me to new places, not of the heart.

I tried to remember "Polonius' Advice to Laertes" a la Hamlet, but I had no luck adhering to those *dicta* anymore than Luther had in keeping his vows. I was trying "this above all, to thine own self be true." St. Paul wrote "nothing can ever separate us from the love of Christ" (Romans 8:38), and it is true. But you don't always feel like it at the time. Soren Kierkegaard said, "Repetition is the joy of life." I suppose that depends upon what you are repeating.

My elder brother Stanley said that I had become an "erudite eremite." Well, I was hiding out, for sure. I clearly remember praying during my bar watches that God would send me a good woman before he found me a good job. Thank goodness, that is exactly what happened!

By now, I was peddling coffee during the day, and tending bar at night. Along came Arlene, who ended my "endless line of romantic splendor." Now I had really "struck gold!" Not "fool's gold" this time. Like C. S. Lewis, God had waited until I was much older to give me the companion of my life, a complete passion of body, mind, and spirit for me to grow into. "I'm lookin' for a heart of gold, and I'm growin' old."

How can anyone explain the meeting of two spirits, out of all the millions of possibilities? When I graduated from High School, Arlene was born the following month. That rather puts it in perspective, and shows the remoteness of the chance. Now this is what I would call one of Kierkegaard's "Moments:" where the vertical meets the horizontal, the divine meets the earthly, the eternal meets the temporal, and the doctrine of "convergence" is finally authenticated.

Arlene was standing outside a wig shop one fine summer's day, comparing strands of hair for her client in the daylight. I had just finished lunch with a friend of mine, and we were standing in the parking lot of the "strip center," chatting away about the good 'ol times in the insurance business. My friend kept looking over my shoulder, and I finally turned around to see what he could see. About a block away stood this inspiring "phantom of delight." He pointed Arlene out to me, and I strolled down to her wig shop on the ruse of selling coffee.

When I entered the store, out came a Dolly Parton look-alike, who owned the shop. After pretending to offer them a coffee service, I asked "Dolly" about the young lady in the back of the store, styling wigs.

The Holy Spirit must have been with me, because I have never made this approach in my life. "That young lady in the back, is she married?" "No." "Is she engaged?" "No." "Then I would like to be formally introduced to her." "Dolly" put me through the same drill, and then she went back to ask Arlene if she would like to be introduced to this strange man at the counter.

Arlene, reluctantly, came forward. I asked if I could call her for lunch sometime. She gave a reticent OK. I waited two full hours before I called. She said "no." I waited two more hours, and called to invite her for dinner the next evening. She said "yes." The rest is a 32-year old history of complete marital bliss. For me.

After she got off, Arlene began coming by to assist me in preparing the condiments for the bar. And there she would stay for hours, dancing the night away and waiting for me to get off work. I would sweat out the night, hoping against hope that Arlene wouldn't fall for one of the hunks she was dancing with while waiting for skinny me to get off work in the wee hours of the morning.

By this time I had "prospered" enough to buy a beat up old Chevy with a bullet hole in the windshield. That had almost put Arlene off from ever seeing me again, as it was the very chariot in which I had picked her up on the first date. But Arlene had great insight and fortitude, and stayed by my side when I was in the black hole, the existential abyss of my life. How and why she peeked into the depths of my soul and saw any promise at all was a complete and welcome mystery to me. Actually, she says, it was to her, too.

The Bible says, "The Word became flesh, and dwelled among us." Well, here it was, all over again. The Word appeared to me in the flesh of Arlene, and it was God's gift for sure. The "flesh" was to become the "Word" again, as you will see. But that's the way it works. It was the "vertical" moment occurring in the "horizontal" plane, just as Socrates and Soren K said it would be. Thus the cycle of life continues: the Word to flesh, and the flesh to Word.

Since I was just emerging from my indigence, and we had dated all of six months, we decided to get married. Arlene had the money ($700.) and I had the time. It proved to be a good financial investment for her, but at the time it was "shock and awe" for her family.

Besides catching Arlene, "the eighth wonder of the world," I got a bonus in her son Damon. After a couple of years, when he was eight years old, we adopted each other, and life began again for me. I had missed out on most of my own sons' teenage years. Here was a chance to provide a stable and loving home for my new son.

Thirty-one years later, it is still a complete and welcome mystery to us. I believe the symphony, "The Planets" by Gustav Holst, and in particular Jupiter, "The Bringer of Jollity," would express my joy as the world began to turn and the sun to shine again.

As to the Elegant Barn, today it is a "Pet Shop." In a way it was then, too.

I wrote a poem for my Christmas card that year:

> *"Leaves have fallen*
> *So have I*
> *Snow is coming*
> *And Winter.*
> *Leaves will blossom*
> *So will I*
> *Love is flowering*
> *And Spring.*

The "Far Country" had brought me home again, when I had "come to my senses." Arlene helped me do that.

CHAPTER 10

THE WAREHOUSE

Pathos

"For even darkness cannot hide God; to you the
night shines as bright as the day. Darkness and
light are both alike to you."

(Psalm 139:11-12)

I can't believe the plethora of megalomaniacal bosses that I have
had over the years. From bishops to pawns, general managers,
vice presidents, and little people who own companies, there's
something about power and people. I have learned along the way
that this kind of behavior is endemic in all corporations,
companies, and business cultures.

Winston Churchill once said, "Megalomania is the only form
of sanity," referring to his domineering method. Maybe I will
someday qualify. Maybe I already have.

After several months of bartending, I decided that perhaps
this was not my ultimate calling in life. I called on several

employment agencies, and one of them had an opportunity that had the promise of something, anything.

After an interview with a friend of the owners, I was hired for $300. per month! That's how desperate I was. I had the high honor of opening a new branch for a company in the office coffee service business. It was another new start situation.

As in my life insurance career, I knew absolutely nothing about coffee, which turned out to be an advantage. The coffee business in general has nothing to do with coffee. It has to do with sales, marketing, pricing, bluffing, and all the fine arts of business. When I began to sell coffee, the price was about 50 cents per pound. Within months, thanks to a "freeze in Brazil," the price escalated to $5.00 per pound.

The coffee industry prospered exponentially, while there was absolutely no shortage of coffee, just as there was no shortage of oil. We all went from Pontiacs to BMW's, and the fact that the price of coffee increased at each monthly delivery was a pain, but eventually accepted by all customers.

The manager assigned to me in the coffee business was totally sphincteresque! He enjoyed calling all of his subordinates "pricks." He would spend hours describing the cupidity and stupidity of his senior partners in the business. I don't think he had ever heard the ancient proverb, "Muzzle not the ox." His favorite "proverb" was, "the shit floats to the top!" Well, he was at the top. That explained everything. He was "world class" in that regard.

After a few months I began to get the hang of procuring new accounts, and that began a twelve-year stint in a business in which I had absolutely no affinity. One of the secretaries whom I hired turned out to have been one of Mick Jagger's girlfriends. Well! She liked to go out and get drunk and seduce other guys, married or unmarried. She came back from a late lunch one day, drunk and happy, and that was the end of her brief career in the coffee business.

The coffee business was several years of hell, but I knew I could overcome if I just hung on until the world turned. And it did. Big time.

It was during this adventure that a most unexpected opportunity presented itself to us. An old spiritual sings "When you're down and out, lift up your head and shout, there's gonna be a great day!" It was back to the beginning.

The timing of heaven touching the earth is strange and mysterious indeed. Without any apparent reason that I can remember, Arlene and I began to attend church. One Sunday a District Superintendent was guest speaker, and mentioned having to go to the little church in Georgetown, California, to fill in. It was just a little, neglected, poverty-stricken church, about to go out of business.

No full-time pastor wanted to, or could afford to, feed a flock of 20-30 people. They had experienced a drought of pastoral leadership. They simply could not afford a "real pastor." So I volunteered to take three Sundays in a row and proclaim the Gospel! The church rolls indicated there were about 80 souls on board, but most were in rest homes or had moved away, or had occupied lots in the local cemetery. Once again, the starting pay was $300. per month. How could I resist that kind of offer?

Georgetown is a small hamlet, nestled among a few other small hamlets, known as the "Georgetown Divide," a territory rising up between two forks of the American River. Coloma, Greenwood, Kelsey, Garden Valley, and Cool, dot the landscape in an area surrounded by scattered homes and farms and ranches of every description, inhabited by many different cultures.

There are bikers and bar bullies, mountain mammas and suburbanites, small business folk and contractors, manual laborers and freeloaders, equestrians and retired elite, foresters and poachers, farmers and vintners, blue collar and professionals, rednecks and rowdies, dedicated drunks and moral models. Pilgrims all. The harvest was ripe.

Once in a while, something called "Mountain Justice" was invoked, which meant that unhappy victims of poaching or other misdemeanors took care of the intruders without benefit of the court system. A man could find himself tied to a tree overnight, after being roughed up a bit.

Now mind you, I hadn't preached a sermon in over 12 years, and had no "barrel" to fall back on. I started sweating great drops of blood to prepare that first sermon. The title?

"What on Earth Are You Looking For?" Rather well received. The second: "What In Heaven Do You Expect?" Okay. The third: "What In Hell Are You Doing?" Hallelujah!

After three divine moments like this, a leader of the church (the town Judge) called the District Superintendent and asked if I could be appointed as part-time pastor. So it was that I was appointed the illegitimate pastor of the Georgetown United Methodist Church. My ordination certificate had not yet been reinstated.

What did I have going for me? Well, it can truly be said that I was now an expert in "sin," and the ways of the world. Actually, I felt that I had a much better perspective on what the average layman was going through, now that I had gone through it all, or a lot of it.

Most "religious people" are all screwed up, and are fighting the same battles as anyone else. When someone leads with the fact that they are a "born again Christian," my shield comes straight up. That little "brand" has been used in a million egregious ways.

St. Paul talked about the fact that all of his weaknesses were, in God's eyes, strengths, and all of his strengths, in God's eyes, were weaknesses. So I guess on that premise I was the perfect candidate to pastor a church again. As Mark Twain used to say, "Every virtue has a defect," and I was a man of many virtues!

I did make the decision to be true to myself, and not "play pastor" to people. Emerson wrote that the world adjusts to one who makes his own statement in his own way. In that fashion I made a few townsfolk adjust to this "irreverent reverend," as I was once categorized in the local newspaper. Another more prolific writer characterized me as a "Man of God." I liked both perspectives. I decided to create my own "milieu."

As I look back, I give thanks I had the Elegant Barn days. I was a Nobody, a "failure," a misfit, jerk, an ass, yet there was something in me that chose to survive.

Meanwhile my beloved wife, Arlene, was in a state of whipsaw emotions. That she loved me was not in question. She said, "Richard, you were meant to preach, but I'm not meant to be a pastor's wife." She had not married a pastor. She had married a coffee salesman/bar tender. Arlene had styled wigs for rising and falling stars at the Sacramento "Music Circus," but was not quite ready for this new culture shock.

Arlene was 18 years younger than I, but looked something like 30 years younger. The flock was bewitched, bothered, and bewildered about the new pastor's wife. Like something out of "The Music Man," the word went forth. I appeared to some as "Professor Harold Hill," and Arlene was "Marian, the Librarian." "Pick a little, talk a little." Her presence was the talk of the town. The skirts of young ladies were worn quite high in those days, and the hair quite long, and Arlene was a sight to behold in her "sizzlers," (dresses with extremely short skirts and panties to match the print.)

Attendance began to pick up speed rather quickly with the new novelty team on board, and Arlene quickly became accepted and admired. It was a gargantuan leap of faith for her, but she made the leap like a ballet dancer. The church was growing so fast, that one of the "little ol' ladies" made a motion at a board meeting: "Let's freeze the membership!" She liked her little ol' church.

Arlene had grown up in a rather large family, and had been placed in the role of surrogate mother (or Cinderella) in terms of housework, cooking, cleaning, and other chores. She was the "stupid" one in the family. There was a reason for that, of which she was totally unaware. She had suffered "the slings and arrows of outrageous fortune."

Arlene had no idea she was dyslexic. She had bought into other's negative opinions of herself as a result. Her low self-esteem was buried alive in her subconscious, and her struggle to blossom into a secure, poised, confident, and capable pastor's wife was somewhat Herculean. But she came shining through, and became teacher, youth leader, puppeteer, counselor, and artist. Her stained glass window creations adorn the Georgetown post office, and many custom homes on the Georgetown Divide. I've always said that 100 years from now, people will say of Arlene, "I think her husband was a preacher."

Now she began to take her destiny into her own hands. Arlene went to college and learned how to "track" words and sentences. Her progress was remarkable, and like Eliza in Pygmalion, she zoomed along in her vocabulary and reading ability. Then she took classes in English and Algebra, and began to feel comfortable facing new information on many fronts.

Arlene blossomed exponentially, and became a true companion and real partner in my ministry and life. I composed a valentine for her, and had a calligraphy artist print it:

"A VALENTINE QUESTION"

"Where is the sun
That shone the day I met you?
  Where the moon
  The night I held your hand?
Where is the star
The night we made the promise?
  Where the falling star
  When we first disagreed?
Where is the place
That we became true lovers?
  When the time
  We had our first embrace?
How could I tell
That I would always love you,
  Whoever knows
  When happiness is found?"

I often say I know more about heaven, and she knows more about the earth. And then she adds, "Yes, but I know more about the earth than you do about heaven!" She does. Arlene is a seamstress (dresses to drapes), interior decorator, chemist, electrician, household engineer, mechanic, architect, artist, epicureanchef, husband tamer, mother and grandmother supreme.

Arlene and I eventually moved to the foothills, bought a home in

Auburn Lake Trails, in Cool, commuted to Sacramento during the week, and served the church on the weekends. I used to enjoy saying that I made an "Honest Living" selling coffee during the week, and was a pastor of a church on the weekends.

During this period Arlene quit work for four years to see Damon through high school. She was his personal chauffeur for all of his athletic endeavors, which included wrestling, track, and football. Damon excelled in every sport in which he participated, and dated the prettiest of the cheerleaders.

There is a certain felicity in being a pastor in a small town, rural, isolated church. We made many close personal friends, and our lives were interwoven with all the human joys, sorrows, sufferings and songs of an ever-expanding social and spiritual life. I was selected to serve on the school board of the Black Oak Mine School District for a couple of years, and learned how to stay awake and make critical decisions regarding the lives of our students until 2:00 o'clock in the morning, a practice which I thought was not always productive.

Slowly and surely the simple Gospel began to flow through my soul, and the basic truths of the parables of Jesus refreshed my spirit. As I prepared for Sunday mornings, the beauty and magnetism of the parables of the lost sheep, the lost coin, the mixing with "trailer trash" that Jesus enjoyed, all had a newer and deeper meaning for me. I had been there, done that. The Good Shepherd had brought me back to the fold.

By this time, I had learned that doctrinal truths had very little relevance to everyday life. The doctrine of the Trinity, the "Apostles' Creed," the great questions and arguments of the ancient church, the middle age refinements of it, the modern theological "heavies," spoke quite an arcane language to the modern pilgrim.

The latest theological thunderbolt shakes the foundations of "Mariolatry." The suggestion is that we might better be praying to Mary of Magadala than to Mary the mother of Jesus. This Mary was a much closer friend and supporter of Jesus. According to the Gospels, Jesus himself had rebuffed his mother and siblings, and preferred the company of "those who do the will of God." His "support group" was primarily women. As the old evangelist would say, "It's in the Book!"

The doctrine of the "Immaculate Conception" in the Catholic tradition has nothing to do with the birth of Jesus. It moves the idea of the "virgin birth" back one generation to the conception of Mary, the mother of Jesus. The idea is to keep sex out of the picture when it comes to holy folk. Keep out sex, keep out sin. One cannot be sinless if sex is involved. That's the idea. Now we have two "virgin births:" Mary and Jesus.

So this "Immaculate Conception" that puzzled me so many years ago as a boy seems to be a "red herring" dreamed up by the church fathers in the 19th century and traditionally elevated Mother Mary over Jesus himself as an object of prayer requests. Saints preserve us! "Deus ex machina"

Saint Martin Luther King, Jr., Saint Socrates, Saint Abe Lincoln and other uncanonized heroes who have laid down their lives for the truth are kept at a distance by a tradition whose ultimate goal is to protect itself from "corruptions."

Meanwhile, back at the front, one of Mother Nature's tricks that she played on me was the passing of a kidney stone. It took about three months for the little bugger to travel through the canal, so I never knew when I would crumple up and fall to the floor in utter agony. Upon occasion, I could feel it coming on while in the pulpit on Sunday mornings. Fortunately, a very talented layman by the name of Fred could take over in a moment's notice, and preach a sermon as good or better than mine, so I could crawl into my car and Arlene could whisk me home. Meningitis provided another episode.

Among the unexpected treats was a jaunt with the Jeepers' Jamboree, during their 25th Anniversary trip up and over the Rubicon. We passed Uncle Tom's Cabin, (where you had to have a beer), then to Loon Lake, where the real four-wheeling starts. On to Spider Lake, to Buck Island Lake, and then through the "Big Sluice," a deep trench of granite boulders, and on to Rubicon Springs, just short of Lake Tahoe.

Hundreds and hundreds of jeeps, creeping and crawling over great granite boulders, maintained by mechanics hovering overhead in helicopters, cavorted for a four day hoot and holler in the great outdoors. It was quite a spectacle.

At the summit of our trip, we were greeted by a band of bagpipers, a parade tromping through the campground of hundreds of tents, and a magnificent steak barbeque with all the trimmings. It was quite a production. It became the prototype for similar events all over the world, and Mark Smith, the "Jeep Master", had catapulted himself from an obscure businessman to a major player in the automotive industry.

One evening, we were the guests of an "aristocratic" family who lived on "Heathen Hill." They had invited, in addition to my holiness, a Catholic Priest (Father Whoever) and his associate, "Brother George" from the Diocese in San Francisco, a PR man for the church. He introduced himself to me as "Brother George," so, in an effort to balance the moment, I introduced myself to him as "Sister Dick!"

Georgetown offered it's share of "non-traditional" weddings. One featured the bride and groom mounted on horseback and riding off into the setting sun. One was under a waterfalls. I could have been reciting the Gettysburg Address and no one would have noticed the difference.

Mountain funerals can also be a little different from time to time. One such was by the South Fork of the American River for a man who, with his "lady," had driven over a huge gulch and was found four days later off Highway 193. We scattered his ashes as we remembered his "wild thing" life, and I tried to pray him into heaven. I thought his chances were pretty good, seeing as how God loves sinners, the thief on the cross, and other misfits.

The most classic memorial service was held on the landscape of the Georgetown cemetery. This soul had been a member of "E Clampus Vitus," a rather arcane group of red-shirted rowdies, who had a strange, ball-testing initiation that lasted for three or four days. The local history books suggest that this burlesque of secret organizations was founded around 1855 by gold miners. The "Poor Blind Candidates" were introduced to "Hog Latin," and other indignities. It was an antidote to pride.

Well, here was one of their champions, about to be planted in the earth forever. The "Head Humbug," at the end of my strained effort at eloquence, got to his feet and yelled to the hundreds of Clampers something like, "Hey, let's give old Charlie a big send-off!" And with that, there were three cheers. No, not cheers. Three "HEE-HAWS!"

The donkey cries thundered through the cemetery, and all the red shirts were in a moment of genuine salute to their dearly departed brother. (Incidentally, their Jackass yells sounded pretty authentic.)

The late Jesuit Catholic priest, Anthony de Mello once said he was going to write a book someday and the title would be "I'm an Ass, You're an Ass." He said, "That's the most liberating, wonderful thing in the world, when you openly admit you're an ass. When people tell me I'm wrong, I say, 'What can you expect from an ass?'" I think he could have been a Clamper!

Life in Auburn Lake Trails was an excursion all in itself. Arlene and I became actors and singers in the theatrical productions. "The Follies" offered a different variety show every few months. Arlene was a big hit as a belly dancer, again stretching the imagination of those who, up to then, had a very limited concept of what or who a preacher's wife should be. A few of the men had difficulty expressing to me their sincere appreciation of Arlene's talent. But you could tell they were grateful.

For my part, I was to appear in a "Big Bird" costume that Arlene constructed for me, and I sang "Yellow Bird." Then Arlene built me a costume that was a combination of a lion and a dog. So, I was a "Lyin' Dog!" I sang Sergeant Kilmer's "Trees," and barked and howled my way into the hearts of future church members, who had never witnessed anything like it.

Arlene took up golf. She took lessons for six months, and practiced every day early in the morning on her way to work. She was offered a lot of free tips from the professionals on the driving range. They admired her determination, natural talent, and other assets. Eventually Arlene began to out-drive me, and, on occasion, outplayed my sons and me. It was sheer delight to see her swing the club and improve her game.

After a few years on the Georgetown Divide, Arlene and I recruited a dozen folk to take a trip to the "Holy Land." We barely managed to take off from an iced-over airport in New York City, but we did make it into Tel Aviv, and the weather was perfect.

It was 1985, and we had the good fortune to visit Israel in a time of relative peace. Our guide Isaac was a wonderfully informed and eloquent speaker. Isaac informed us that the original names for Jesus and Mary were "Yeshua" and "Miriam." The names we know are Greek.

Isaac moved us through the centuries of Israel, captive of one nation after the other. Thanks to the productivity of the Kibbutz, the land looked very similar to the San Joaquin Valley. Swamplands had been reclaimed and turned into fertile fields.

From Tel Aviv we went up to Netanya, the home of a "wholesale" diamond factory. Here we mortgaged a small part of our future and procured Arlene's first significant diamond.

Then it was up to Caesarea, over to Caesarea Philippi, and south to the Sea of Galilee, where we enjoyed a day cruise, and a stopover at a seaside restaurant. They served us something called "St. Peter's Fish," which was barely edible.

We took in many of the sites that Constantine's mother Helena had christened in the fourth century as authentic. Here is where this happened. There is where that happened. But of course there were differing traditions, Catholic and Protestant, so it was up to the pilgrim to decide which was what. Two sites for the birth of Christ, two for the Last Supper, two for the crucifixion, two for the tomb, it was tea for two all over the place.

Of course, the still untamed power of mischief was managing to surge up inside of me, even in the "Holy Land." We came to the Dome of the Rock in downtown Jerusalem, the traditional site of Solomon's Temple, and now the third most venerated shrine in Islam, it being the site where the Prophet Muhammad commenced his mystical ascent into heaven. We were instructed to leave cameras, recorders, and any technical appurtenances outside the Temple before entering.

Not I. I tucked my mini-recorder in my pocket and entered

the Holy Shrine. I wanted to capture the narration of the Muslim priest so I could refresh my memory upon our return home. And wouldn't you know? A great Temple guardian all garnished in glorious robes, about eight feet tall, came and stood right next to me, closer than my beloved Arlene.

I could not click off my recorder without alerting my personal bouncer. I didn't know how much tape there was left before it would reach the end. If it reached the end, a high squeal would betray my transgression, and it would be off with my head! I don't think I would have been greeted in "Paradise" with a selection of virgins. I haven't the foggiest where that tape is today, or if it recorded anything. Only Allah knows! But I still shudder to think what kind of fool I was. Another very close call!

Sitting by the Sea of Galilee, we took comfort in knowing that somewhere nearby Jesus had stepped into Peter's boat, and preached to the multitudes. The Garden of Olives still grew, and you could eyeball the landscape and know that Jesus probably did see the Roman soldiers with their bright torches marching straight towards him in the middle of the night. He stood his ground, when he could easily have escaped, and the rest is "reliable history."

Toward the end of our trip, we ended up in a hotel in downtown Jerusalem. I came down with a massive case of the flu, and was bedridden for two or three days. My good friend Noel LeRoque had brought a small band of pilgrims to join with us. Arlene didn't want to miss seeing Masada, so Noel and our new friend, Dr. Marvin, graciously consented to accompany her on the way.

The second evening in my hotel room, the phone began to ring. A voice said, "I want to speak to Gloria." I replied, in a very weak voice, "There is no Gloria here," and hung up the phone. A few minutes later, the phone rang again, with the same request, insisting that I was hiding Gloria.

About a half hour later, Noel came into my room, and I explained my plight. The phone rang. Noel answered. In response to the caller's accusation that Gloria was probably hiding under my bed, Noel got down on his hands and knees, took a peek under the bed, and said in his best authoritarian voice, "Sir, I'm looking under the bed. There is no Gloria in this room!" That was that. But the "mystery of Gloria" remains unsolved.

Of course, the whole idea of a trip to the "Holy Land" is rather foolish. Looked at from a truly Biblical or wholesome theological perspective, the whole world is the Holy Land. Why do we take trips to try to find it? The idea is that all of life is sacred. Every place is a shrine, and every moment a Mecca.

Somewhere along the way in Georgetown I was re-legitimized as an ordained pastor. I had been "frocked", "de-frocked", ("voluntary location") and "re-frocked." I have a most unusual set of ordination papers that are framed in my office, in which I take a certain curious pride. I was an authentic member of the clergy, once again, with full powers to baptize, marry, bury and serve the sacrament of communion. I cherished those moments more now than I had before.

Annual Conference sessions were still on a rampage about social issues. I think my problem had to do with the "wisdom" that was employed in arriving at the resolutions. The Conference was comprised, for the most part, of amateurs in the arena of politics, science, environment, justice, and other "causes." I was simply not as sure as the "Body" was about what to do. I find it hard to trust "clergy in the bulk."

The fact that certain "issues" had to be addressed seemed more than apparent. But "justice" is a regional concept. One region's justice is another region's injustice. By now the church was "top heavy" with General Boards and Agencies and the "slicks" who ran them and expensive publications promoting their agendas. The cost of all this bears down on the local churches, already bravely facing economic hardship, and wondering why the economy is shrinking, and the "apportionments" are growing. "When will we ever learn?"

I know the ancient proverb. "It is easier to curse the darkness than to light a candle." But the loss of millions of parishioners nationally during a population explosion should speak for itself.

It seems to me that we might avail ourselves of the expertise of those in the areas of concern, pros and cons, rather than listen to self-anointed experts on the subjects.

Among the most infantile resolutions was one about world population. One of our colleagues stood up, without having gone to a "Section Meeting" to massage the issue, and gave an alarming speech about how the world would be doomed if we didn't soon curb propagation. So his motion was to challenge all United Methodists to quit having so many babies. Hallelujah!

It was righteousness by resolution all over again. The motion passed unanimously. I have no idea what impact it had, if any, on the sexual habits of Methodists. All I knew was that I, personally, had had a vasectomy, so my social consciousness was pure as the driven snow. That was a first. Maybe the only.

All along the way I maintained an insatiable thirst for reading. Now it was books on tape during my weekday business commutes, and real books. History, biography, psychology and classics, with a few novels. I read the eleven volumes of "The Story of Civilization" by Will and Ariel Durant, Churchill's books, biographies of the famous and infamous, "Great Books," and not so great. Of course Micheners' serial historical novels. It was like eating candy. I think the "Diary of a Napoleonic Foot Soldier" sort of put life in true perspective. It was better than Homer.

I bought a Yamaha organ, and my childhood piano lessons from the Greek goddess still resonated in the archives of my brain, so I enjoyed making new joyful noises on the high tech "calliope."

CHAPTER 11

SERENDIPITY

ETHOS

"Trust God from the bottom of your heart; don't try to figure out everything on your own . . . He will direct you and crown your efforts with success."

Proverbs 3:4 (Peterson: The Message)

Son Dan went back to Oklahoma several years ago to my hometown. He was in his early twenties. He called me from there and thanked me. For what? For moving to California! It was more prophetic than any of us could imagine.

He probably remembered the time we returned to Holdenville for a family visit, and were having lunch at a local café. We happened to lift up a water glass and beheld a swarm of minerals and other substances floating in the glass. We called the server over and shared our plight. She held up the glass and, upon inspection, turned on her heels and shouted back to the kitchen,

"Change the dishwater!" It was real down home. Of course, that could happen anywhere. This waitress just had flair about her.

The original "reason" I moved to Sacramento did prove to be completely irrelevant. Sacramento was to be a door to surprising and fulfilling adventures. What followed was to be an extreme blessing for my family and me, and could not have been foreseen. Ah, sweet mystery of life.

So by then I was in my fifties, I owned a home with a least $5,000 equity, and had a couple of hundred dollars in "savings." My financial clock was ticking faster and faster, and my balance sheet was teetering on the edge of disaster.

I have two theology degrees, a record of church building, a marathon in life insurance sales, a brilliant career as a mixologist, and a pioneer in coffee sales. What should I do? *"The Moving Finger writes; and having writ, moves on; nor all your Piety nor Wit shall lure it back to cancel half a line, nor all your tears wash out a word of it."* *(Fitzgerald)* We cannot erase the past, but it is always transformable.

During my bartending days, when I was "foot loose and fancy free" to go anywhere and start anew, my decision to stay in the capitol city of California was to prove most fortuitous. In a classic case of "Serendipity," an unexpected door opened.

Son Stan became a route driver in the coffee business, much to the dismay of his mother and other close friends. He was offered "counseling," but had the good sense and great self-esteem to decline that proposition, and make his own leap of faith. He jumped into one of the coffee vans, and life was never the same for him again.

We had both been warned by our pompous general manager "never to cross him," (as he spun on his heels in a bar room), so with that encouragement we decided on a "sting operation."

One of our coffee customers was in the esoteric business of document retrieval, among other ventures. My son took a liking to the secretary of their over-leveraged enterprises, and they became good friends. The business of her employers was disintegrating, and the young lady decided, with our encouragement, to open a similar business, and a new partnership was born. It was another new start for me.

During my coffee debacle, I managed to fund this son (thanks to a small loan from Mom) and his by now fiancé into the business of document retrieval. It's not an easy endeavor to describe, but we fetched public records from the Secretary of State and other public agencies, on behalf of bankers, lawyers, financial institutions, escrow companies, and other interested parties. It's called "Public Record Research." "Search West" was our new *nom de guerre.*

Son Stan proved to have the "Midas touch," and we made very good connections all across the nation. The business grew and grew, with clients and correspondents scattered over all the major states. I did my part by flying around the country scooping up new customers. In eight years we had built the largest search company west of the Mississippi, and employed forty souls.

After 8 years, an offer came out of the blue from Prentice Hall Legal and Financial Services, alias Simon-Schuster Publishing, alias Paramount, alias Viacom, to buy our business. They wanted to build a conglomerate of information services, and we were one of a half-dozen companies they bought that year.

In 1987 we relented, and allowed them to buy us out of business, and we "merged." In the process, I was hired by the new owners to be the "Managing Director" of the "National Seminar Division" of "Prentice Hall Legal and Financial Services." Holy Toledo! My resume was really growing.

In this role I traveled all across the nation for three years, speaking to groups of lawyers, paralegals, bankers, lenders, lessors, escrow officers, and others, explaining the access and application of public records. I wrote articles in national paralegal and legal secretary magazines.

In the November 1989 issue of "The Docket," the international journal of the "National Association of Legal Secretaries," I wrote an article entitled "The Mystery House of Local Records." My analogy was the Winchester Mystery House in San Jose, California, a mansion of 160 rooms, "where doors open to blank walls, stairs lead up to nowhere, rooms exist without windows, and corridors lead to dead ends." The simile also applies to theology schools, or churches, or synagogues, or mosques. They are all "Winchester Cathedrals," with the same labyrinthine interiors and arcane wisdom and blind alleys.

Thanks to our newfound "wealth," Arlene and I were able to build our dream home on a hill in Auburn Lake Trails. On a site of 14 acres, we could view the snow-capped Sierras, stroll through our very own Black Oak Forest, and capture wildlife on our camcorder. Arlene spent hours designing our new nest, and enjoyed massaging and tweaking every square inch of the two-story castle. Then she designed and built a stained glass window of a miner prospecting on a creek-side for the entry by the front door. It was stunning. Still is. The world was our oyster, and she was the pearl.

We have a wonderful photograph of Arlene standing on the hill below the house, with the walls towering behind her, and her arms raised straight out in embrace of the whole world. She was spiritually levitating. It was as impressive to us as the castle of Neuschwanstien in Germany, through which we had strolled.

Our brief elation was shattered by tragedy. For every gain, it seems, there is a loss. During this period one of our grandsons, Ryan, slipped, fell and drowned in a spa in his backyard. At age one and ½, Ryan left us, in spite of the tremendous efforts of his parents and the emergency response team and the doctors. It was a very dark night of the soul for all of us.

At the graveside, son Dan began to speak softly to Ryan's mother in the most eloquent fashion. Calm, strong, loving, hopeful and assuring images came flowing from his mind into verbal expression. I was standing right behind him so that I could hear what he was saying before the pastor began to speak.

I have preached many a sermon in an effort to comfort the bereaved, but none so straight and true as Danny's by his son's grave. I was so grateful to have a son that could plow his way through his grief and sorrow, and into visions of hope and faith for Ryan and for us all.

My good friend Robert van der Toorren, mentioned above, sent me a comforting poem, written by Joost van den Vondel in 1630. It was a poem to his wife on the occasion of the death of their little boy, "Constantijntje." Rob translated it from the Dutch in October, 1987.

"Little Constantin,
Hallowed Youngster,
Cherub —

From above he smiles
With a mirthful eye
At the vanities here below.

Mother — says he –
Why do you cry?
Why do you sob
Upon my corpse?

Up here I live
Up here I soar:
A cherub of the Firmament –

Up here I sparkle
And I drink what the pourer
Of all good
Serves the souls
That revel here:
Frolicsome in great profusion –

So then:
Learn to travel
In thought
To palaces
Out of the mire
Of this whirling world –

ETERNITY TRANSCENDS MOMENT –

Arlene and I funded a trust for a scholarship at Damon's high school in Ryan's memory. It is called the "Triangle of Competence" award, given to a student that the faculty selects each year. The three points of the qualifying triangle were skills, knowledge, and attitude.

In a strange twist a few years later, I was attending a national sales meeting of Prentice Hall. The president and his staff wanted to offer an award to the outstanding sales person of the year. They called me in to participate in the hurried meeting. They had no idea how to frame such an award.

So I borrowed from our experience with Ryan and the scholarship, and suggested and explained the "Triangle of Competence" award. It was immediately accepted, and I was left in the room with the Vice President of Sales to "coach" him in the presentation that evening.

I began to flesh out the concept. I didn't get very far. After every word or two I said, the Vice President broke in and asked, "How do you spell that?" It took us about two hours to frame the five minute presentation. To this day I can't figure out why he wanted the correct spelling of every other word, because no one was going to read his little speech except him. Sometimes I wonder where Vice Presidents and other corporate officers come from.

On a happier note, one day, with grandson Levi and dog "Tiffer" looking out from our 35-foot high bay window in Cool, a den of foxes appeared just below our home. They took residence in a large drain tunnel clearly in view, and the kits romped and played like little kittens, running into each other and tumbling down the hill, while Momma and Poppa fox looked on. As we were recording, a couple of deer strolled through the scene, between the foxes, and fox and deer ignored each other, and life went on. It was as near heaven as we had ever sensed. Was Ryan watching, too? Life is a bittersweet waltz.

CHAPTER 12

THE HOMECOMING

KAIROS

"We're going to have a wonderful time. My son
is here, given up for dead, and now alive!"
Luke 15:24 (Peterson: The Message)

When we left the Georgetown church, the townsfolk orchestrated a wonderful send-off in the local gymnasium. Songs and skits encapsulated high moments, and memorable episodes were recalled. One of the "little old ladies" kept me from soaring too high, as she stood up and said, "In spite of everything, Dick, you're OK!"

The high point for me was a declaration by one of my friends: "Dick knows how to motivate, delegate, and celebrate!"

After having served the Georgetown church, part-time, for fifteen years, I received a call from my new District Superintendent. "Dick, how would you like to start up another new church?" Another new start?

I had just retired from Prentice Hall, now 60 years of age, and ready to start "living the dream." I was "burnt out" from the travel and pressure of "corporate intrigue," working "eight days a week" between weekend church and weekday travel, and eager for a real sabbatical.

But here was an offer I couldn't refuse. It meant that my commute from Auburn Lake Trails to the new church would be doubled, my church salary would be cut in half, and we could start all over again in a schoolhouse.

I was to be given six months "leave" before being appointed to active duty. Three months later I received a call from the "founding pastor" that he wanted to quit early, and couldn't I start in September rather than January?

Sure, but I hadn't yet rested and recovered. Four months into the project I contracted a monstrous case of the "shingles." I was told it would be a combination of stabbing pain that would evolve into a rash that would produce unbearable itching sensations. I never got to the itching.

I felt as though an electric frying pan had been placed in my left armpit, turned to high, and left on. The stabbing pain was relentless, and I survived only with the help of a drug called percodan for over six months, and then lesser painkillers beyond that for another six months. My doctor suggested I might be getting "high" or becoming addicted. But I wasn't "high," I was just trying to get "even." Most shingles patients recover within weeks, but I must have drawn the long (or short) straw.

In twelve months I downgraded my medications from percodan to darvocet to vicodin to Tylenol to nothing at all. To this day I still experience a reduced degree of constant stabbing pain, relentless, from my left shoulder blade around my under arm to my left breast. My only painkiller now is a couple of beers in the evening.

The challenge at "Sierra Pines United Methodist Fellowship" (it wasn't an official church, yet) took many shapes and forms. There was a small cross section of ages, interests, talents, and gifts. We were one small happy family, especially with a children's program called "Logos."

Logos was a well-designed study session, enhanced by games and food and craft activity, and nurtured by active parents who participated in an three-hour evening program once a week. From that program we built a strong kid's choir, which charmed the California-Nevada Annual Conference session with robust songs.

Then we got to the building stage. Everyone brought to the table a different perspective, dream, agenda, and plan. There were tough decisions to be made, and people got bruised in the process. St. Paul had his problems with his little churches. He treated them in a forthright fashion, and I'm sure he "lost members."

In spite of many setbacks, false starts, dashed hopes, unexpected barriers, we came together and prevailed over all obstacles. We even got into the "Social Justice" part of our Methodist heritage, in that we offered support to the local food closet ministries, and had other direct involvement extending helping hands and services to individuals and families.

We had our great moments and high epiphanies. There was the stage in the school gymnasium, where our little band of pioneers was swallowed up in space. On "Pet Sunday," we had dogs and cats in attendance, and even a snake, a python! Oh what fun!

Then we moved into what the young people called "the dumb old office building." They were right! The flock was split in two by a half wall that ran through our "chapel," so only the pastor had a view of the whole congregation.

Finally, we had a plan and a builder (Arlene's brother Marland, who saved us over $200,000) and enough money to stake our claim and erect an edifice on the high hill, overlooking the high school. Son Damon did a large share of the construction. We had a beautiful unobstructed view of the golf course at Lake of the Pines. It was sooo beautiful that the Mormons made us a fantastic offer if we would sell to them, but we stood our ground, if you'll pardon the expression.

The last few months were a marathon of challenges from all city and county and public agencies: PG&E, NID, DOT . . . it was an alphabet soup of power-brokers who all wanted their say in how and when we should be granted the right to meet in our little chapel on the hill.

Then came more fun from within. A few well-intentioned folk, who wanted things their way and now, summoned their literary talents and became "letter writers." They managed to keep the pot stirred and rumors flying. I recalled the quote from Shakespeare's Othello: "Who steals my purse steals trash . . . . but he that filches from me my good name robs me of that which enriches not him, and makes me poor indeed."

Love must have prevailed over the "issue" folk, because a fine structure and a happy family now occupy the envious hilltop acreage that is the home of Sierra Pines United Methodist Church.

Overall, we made deep and lasting friendships that continue to enhance and enrich our lives today.

The traditional church has always had its liturgical seasons: Advent, Christmas, Lent, Eastertide, Pentecost, Kingdomtide, etc. Most lay people haven't the foggiest about the origin and meaning of many of these "seasons," and which color and litany is appropriate. The "tides" are irrelevant, except to the privileged professional, or the dedicated seeker, mostly for pedantic reasons.

Perhaps the church should adopt a new series of "seasons:" the Season of Spiritual Birth, the Season of Adolescence, the Season of Bewilderment, the Season of Maturity, the Season of Depression, the Season of Jubilation, the Season of Patience, the Season of Humiliation, the Season of Disobedience, the Season of Awareness, the Season of Forgiveness, the Season of Love. We could build a whole new litany for these "Seasons," and they might be more pragmatic and healing than those which are currently celebrated.

Life is full of beginnings and pilgrimages and crucifixions and resurrections. Why should the difficulties and differences surprise us? As Anthony de Mello wrote of himself, "What can you expect of an ass?"

CHAPTER 13

PASTOR'S POTPOURRI

SALVOS

"The wage of a good person is exuberant life!"
Proverbs 10:16 (The Message)

Moments are all we have, or that have us. Soren Kierkegaard was right about that. The life of a pastor brings many incredible episodes to the study and into the homes. The variety of unexpected moments is astonishing.

A

I recall the day that a good friend of mine and I visited a man who was experiencing "visitations" from ghosts or spirits, all about his house and ranch. These were not of the friendly variety. He was scared and deeply concerned.

In the light of his ethnic roots and religious background, he gave them a good deal of credence. He was a very troubled spirit. "Billy" lived in a very remote spot off Highway 49. His wife had died recently, and he was surrounded with his children and large responsibilities.

My good lady friend Tati and I went to his home to "clean house." Tati said that in her homeland (Cuba) the preferred "holy water" was coconut water. Since that was not available, I took some natural spring holy water, and we sat down at his dining table.

Billy said that the demons attacked him more often when he was reading the Bible. After a brief prayer for success in our exorcism, we asked him where it was he saw the demons.

There was a large picture window near the table, looking out over the vast wasteland which was his backyard. "There's one now!" he said, pointing to the window. The demon appeared to him as a large black bird with huge wings and the head of a man.

We went outside and began to sprinkle "holy water" in the direction of the flight of the spirit. We traveled from backyard to side yard to front, casting away the evil creatures. Wherever he "saw" a spirit, around the house or inside, we "chased" them all away. Tati told him, "Next time you read the Bible, tell Satan that he can't keep you from it."

Billy came to church next Sunday and was baptized with Tati kneeling beside him. He gave a generous gift of money to our church, and went off to the Philippines to find a new wife. We never saw him again. Tati and I still enjoy the moment we played "Ghost Busters," with the best of intentions. Tati's cousin later told her, "You should have used fresh basil!"

B

Another high moment was as a marriage counselor. A good friend and member of the church came to my house one day, and said he was thinking of leaving his wife. He described the charms of his new love, and then I asked if she felt the same way about him.

No, she wasn't sure at all. So, in my best professional and insightful manner I said, "Joe, you're just being a jerk!" Well, it worked.

He left, is still married to his first true love, but didn't speak to me for several years. I guess I hurt his feelings. "Tough love" has a price.

C

Then there was the day that I was in my study, and a young, disturbed man came into my office. "I just fucked a sheep." I had heard by now the catch phrase that covers a multitude of "sins," the "alternative lifestyle." But he was serious. He was depressed.

What do you say to a very young man with a confession like that? "How was it?" Or, "Jesus can cure you of such desires?" Or "How do you feel about that?" "You're OK, the sheep is OK?"

He was a desperate soul, and died young. Did he go to hell? I don't think so. He was already living in hell. Mother Nature had given him too many cross signals to filter out. If you think he went to hell, then I think you're screwed up. You have just "screwed the pooch" theologically speaking.

D

The decision to pull life support from a dearly loved spouse, parent, or other close relative is a tough one. At the time this decision was finally reached, the family stood together in a large circle, and asked me to pray. The words began to reach my tongue, and the prayer seemed to be of extreme comfort to the family members. I had not prepared for this moment, but the prayer lasted almost four or five minutes. The Bible says that we should not worry when we pray. The right words would come and be given to us. That was surely the case in this instance.

I have often held the hands of dying people, and sometimes at the very moment of death. One moment their spirit resides in their bodies. The next moment there is only silence. I once held the hand of an elderly woman at the moment she died in the hospital. Her daughter was by her side. We had a long, silent prayer, we hugged, and she has always cherished the moment. Those moments transcend all the other stuff pastors endure.

On the other hand, I prayed by the side of another dying woman. She knew that she had only days yet to live. So I offered the most eloquent assurance of which I was capable, and then leaned over her gaunt face to kiss her cheek. When I was very close, she whispered, "You know, Dick, I don't really believe in all that stuff!" I stole silently away.

E

About midway in my return to the pastoral ministry, a colleague of mine and his wife invited us over to dinner. In a moment when we were alone, he confided in me that he was bisexual. I don't know why he picked me out, unless he thought that I had "gay eyes," as a college student once told me. I took it as a tacit invitation for romance, but ignored the offer.

He went on to instruct me that if I weren't bisexual, then I ruled out half the world's population to love! Now I know that love "is a many splendored thing," but I had trouble with his logic. I couldn't even get around to a fraction of the half of the human race I had chosen. Eight billion people. So little time. I have many male friends that I truly love, but I never gave a thought to sharing an orgasm with them.

The "Holy Union" thing still mystifies me. What shall we call the other unions? "Marriage" seems quite a bland sobriquet up against "Holy Union." God bless us everyone.

F

Then there was the great "Rededication Sunday" at Georgetown. This was a once-in-a-long-time chance for the "old faithful" folks to come up to the altar and renew their vows of loyalty to Christ. The hymn was sung several times to give a chance for all to come forward, and it was going very well. The altar was packed and people were standing in the aisles.

Then it happened. One young lady of a Pentecostal background was in attendance. She felt that Methodists were only about ½ way on their way to heaven, because of their lack of enthusiasm, and some of their secular habits. When she saw all those Methodists come forward and praise God, it was too much for her tender heart. She came right up to the altar and fainted "dead away." She was "slain in the spirit." It stopped the music, stopped the service, and all mouths dropped open and astonishment was the order of the day.

We had to put the worship service in suspended animation while her husband was fetched from his home. He entered the chapel and went up to his supine wife, and whispered words of reassurance to her. She began to show signs of life again, and was raised up to normal life once more. Hallelujah! Most of us had never seen anything like it, or been close to it. The episode didn't seem to alter our behavior, or our style of subdued worship. But we had rubbed shoulders with a visitation from something far beyond our meager comprehension.

G

In more light-hearted moments, I recall the band of drinking buddies who came up from the former "Palomino Room" in Sacramento (our "Cheers") to attend Easter services in Georgetown. These guys and gals all went into shock when they heard that I had decided to go back into the pastoral ministry. So they conspired to descend on one of my worship services, in order to fulfill the proverb that "seeing was believing," and to test my resolve.

Thus a convoy of RV's filed up Highway 49 on a Saturday night to enjoy the revelry that mountain retreats promised, and spent the night in something besides prayer and meditation to prepare themselves for this holy pilgrimage.

Hung-over, but true friends, they filed into the little wooden pews and filled three rows. When I asked them to stand and introduce themselves, they did pretty well. One good doctor, however, turned to introduce his current lady, and couldn't remember her name!

He blushed, she helped him, and the service continued.

I "preached" about the parallel between the brilliant poem ("Freedom Train"), Abraham Lincoln's funeral train, and the episodes that immediately followed the resurrection of Jesus. It was well received by my friends "of the bar."

H

Sitting at a table among church friends having dinner, the subject arose as to whether it was better to mount the toilet paper roll forwards or backwards against the wall. I suggested forward was more user friendly, but our host insisted that backwards saved paper! Of course it's really a question of how many panels you use per swipe, but this was not addressed. The fact that Europeans generally wad the paper was interjected, but then we went on to dessert. It's just another example of how church work covers you from beginning to end! Home rituals are just as important as church rituals.

It was as anomalous as when the Rotary Club invited Joe Conforte of the infamous "Mustang Ranch" to speak. Joe brought with him a couple of "customer service representatives" to dinner for a question and answer period. Some of the questions the Rotarians asked of the CSR's were enough to leave the hookers with their mouths open. Life was good. But it was balanced by the days of silent treatment the members received when they returned to their homes.

I

I have had the honor of presiding over the "funeral" services for judges, bartenders, losers and winners. Among the most unusual mountain memorial services was for Charlie. Charlie was up in years, but owed his advanced physical condition mostly to booze. He had also developed a very special language, which he perfected on the golf course. I would call it "creative theology" because of his constant references to the Almighty during his frustrations and sufferings on the golf course from tee to green.

Charlie loved animals. He was a movable "lost and found" for stray cats and dogs. He would come home with a load of strays, take care of them, find new homes for them, or just keep them around. Whenever he played golf, a "litter" of kittens would meet him on the fifth tee, because he always carried a little bag of treats for them.

Charlie loved animals so much that he sometimes illegally fed the deer. On one occasion, he was taking a nap near the woodshop. The deer came along, saw him, kneeled down, and prayed for him to wake up so that he would feed them. At least 20 bucks and does were present and accounted for by an onlooker.

Charlie was a very talented carpenter, and made a thousand things for folks around town who needed a special homemade widget. He once made us a portable platform on which to place our television set. It made a perfectly snug fit into our built in entertainment center.

Charlie was buried near his woodshop. The ashes were placed on the ground (no urn) next to the shop. This site was chosen for it was the very place, the hallowed resting ground of Charlie's wife, whom he had divorced and remarried on several occasions.

All of his friends gathered, had a beer, and poured a portion of it over Charlie's residuum.

Charlie's friend Tom took the liberty of pouring two beers over the abundantly splashed ashes, because the last thing Charlie had said to Tom, when Tom suggested he would have a beer, Charlie responded, "Have two beers for me." That was our version of "Mass" for the day, and I think it was more heartfelt and significant than many of the more traditional masses. We didn't hold a "wake," for there was little hope that Charlie would wake up.

J

Two "great moments" come to mind in Georgetown. The first was the day I was preaching a profound sermon, paralleling the poem by Hermann Haggerdorn, "The Bomb That Fell on Hiroshima," to the "bomb" of Jesus blasting through the ancient Judean culture.

When I reached the part in the poem about a bomb going off, "Barroom!" A loud sound startled the whole flock. The pews in this historical church are made of wood. They have been supporting the supporters for a hundred years. The nails that secure the pews are amazing, in that they have held their own over those years, and an unknown number of holy bottoms, supporting minds and hearts that were deep in prayer and meditation.

The two largest believers in my congregation occupied this particular pew that morning of "Hiroshima". When I said the word "bomb" the nails in that pew gave up the ghost, and a piercing snap shot up and blasted the silence. The pew held, but the moment was impressive. I went on with my brilliant essay, and everyone smothered his or her delight over the timing.

The other moment was in my eloquent message about how God speaks to us. I held an unconnected telephone in my hand, and was making the point about how we need to be "plugged in" in order to hear from God. As I lifted up the phone to display the cord going nowhere, the phone rang! No. Not my phone, but the phone in the study, just behind the rear pew. It was a loud ring, and close in proximity. The flock thought it was a setup. It was incredible timing, and we all laughed and enjoyed the blessings of the Spirit.

K

As a "Maverick Methodist Minister" I had to create my own culture, as I was not about to compromise my integrity and play the "righteous" game, or buy into the "party line" of the hierarchy. So I lived my life in the open. The "beer drinking pastor" was a novelty to many, and a bane to the conservative constituents. I gave them A+ for their tolerance of me.

But I had friends "in low places" as the song goes. I made friends in the "Milestone Bar" in Cool, and treasured their friendship. Some of them were spotted in church on Sundays, a rare sight in those days and lives. We were "friends," as Jesus called his dysfunctional disciples. You might have thought I enjoyed eating and drinking with sinners. You'd be right. Some of my favorite "pagan" friends whose company I truly enjoyed I dubbed the "righteous rascals."

L

"Now in those days," as it is usually written, in Carmel-By-The-Sea, the township is rumored to have hired a "lure" to stroll the beaches, hoping to attract and ensnare "queers." This was the fabulous fifties, and that was the prevalent attitude.

One of my church officers enjoyed the unhappy condition of being a closet homosexual, as we then referred to them. He was caught in the trap one fine sunny day on Carmel beach, and hauled off to the county jail in Salinas. When I got the news, I hastened over to Salinas to see if I could offer any comfort to him.

A cyclone fence enclosed the prison yard, so you didn't have to gain entrance through a gate or door. I could stroll right up to the fence and spot my unlucky friend, and talk around the reason for his little visit to the county jail.

I asked him if I could get him anything, and he said he would appreciate a pack of cigarettes and a magazine. Away I went and retrieved same, and squeezed them through an opening in the fence. He was most appreciative, and we remained good friends.

A friend of mine later asked me what would happen to him. I replied, "I guess they'll ostracize him." She responded, "Well, won't they have to get his permission!"

M

In the fall of '99 my oldest brother Stanley was seriously ill. He had undergone his second major bypass surgery, and was still on the ventilator after two months. I waited until the tube was removed, and caught the next flight to Oklahoma City. Leaving from Sacramento, we had to change planes in Burbank, a most unappealing terminal, to go on to Phoenix and Oklahoma City.

I sat at the rear of the plane. There were two sets of three seats facing each other. A gentleman sat opposite me on my left at the aisle, then an empty middle seat, and then a pretty blonde lady facing me on my right at the window. I was the only one on my row looking at them, so we could each put our feet up on the seat in front of us.

Before take-off, the woman in the window seat began to fidget and fret and tremble with a "textbook fear of flying." I said to her, "What's the matter, don't you go to church?" She said, "Yes I do. I'm an Assembly of God, but it's not working." I responded, "Well, I'm a Methodist, and that doesn't always work for me either!"

I took hold of one of her feet, which was shoeless, resting beside me, and began to rub her foot. I told her not to look out the window until we were airborne, and just to tell me a little about herself. She began to speak non-stop about being a hairstylist living in Norman, Oklahoma, and a thousand other things.

She was most pleasant. After we were up in the air a few minutes, she reached over and took hold of my feet and massaged them all the way to Phoenix! It's the only way to fly! It was far better than first class. I had no idea I was going to have a flight like that when I went back to comfort my brother. I suppose God was rewarding me in advance.

It just goes to show that Pentecostals and Methodists and others can all get along.

Little David sang, "Lord, you know when I sit or stand. When far away you know my every thought." (Psalm 139:2)

N

It was a beautiful morning at the Georgetown amphitheatre. An Easter Sunrise service had drawn a generous, sleepy eyed crowd. It was time for the scripture lesson. The Lay Reader got up to the stage, nuzzled in next to the microphone, and began the lesson. It was about King Saul's rage against young David, his anointed successor to the throne.

At the peak of Saul's rage, he lashed out at David something like "You offspring of a female canine!" That would have been the King James Version. But my dear reader had brought a modern translation, and said these words very slowly, with dramatic spaces in between: "You son of a bitch." The congregation came up out of their early morning trance. They had no idea the Bible could be so interesting.

O

Weddings. It's the ring thing. During one lovely wedding in the outdoors in the mountains in the fall, I held up the ring to make my profound observation about the significance of the ring. Just as I was concluding my remarks, the ring slipped out of my fingers and onto the ground and into the autumn leaves. We took a "ring break," and conducted a search for the prize. The sun was setting, but, at the last moment the ring was found and the ceremony was completed.

Another wedding was held on the deck of a remote mountain resort. The decking was built with half inch spaces in between the planks, and the deck was about three feet off the ground. I held up the ring to make my statement, and the ring popped out of my fingers onto the deck. It bounced to and fro for what seemed like a long time, and my worst fears had to do with the spaces in the deck. But a small lad came to my rescue and grabbed the ring before it disappeared into the darkness below.

I am thinking of giving up handling the ring. Why did God design us to drop things, and to misplace things? It goes on everyday, along with computer glitches.

P

There were many other troubled and broken spirits that came my way, too many to recall. Because of the broken periods of my life, I understood, empathized, and once in a while I was helpful. I was there for them, and many thanked me for that. I thanked them for letting me try.

Once, while strolling through a guided tour of the Beringer Vineyard in Napa Valley, our guide paused to explain why she believed their grapes were superior. "We tend to water our vineyards sparingly, because stressed grapes produce the best wine!" Now I understood why God stresses our "spiritual grapes" now and then.

One of the milestone stories in the Judaic tradition is the parting of the Red Sea. As everyone knows, Moses led the Israelites out of Egypt, and the Pharaoh changed his mind and chased them in hot pursuit. Just at the last moment, as in any good story, the Red Sea parted, allowing the Jews to cross, and then it closed over and destroyed the Egyptian army, and you know the rest of the story. Well, up to now, at least. It is still being written.

There have been so many "Red Sea Partings" in my life that I have lost count. Just at the last moment of a cliffhanging scenario, I have crossed over the sea of trials and impending disaster into a land of milk and honey. Deliverance is a constant reoccurrence in my life.

Q

The exercise of writing this divertimento reminds me of a little ditty my Dad taught me:

> *"King David and King Solomon led merry, merry lives;*
> *With many, many lady friends, and many, many wives;*
> *But when old age crept over them, with many, many qualms,*
> *King Solomon wrote the Proverbs,*
> *And King David wrote the Psalms."*
>
> *(James Naylor)*

All through the different passages of my life, good times and bad, I had a little saying that simply rolled out of my mouth. "And then I wrote a book." Well, here it is, for better or for worse.

Everyone should write an autobiography. It doesn't matter whether it gets read or not. It's a good investment in reflection on the meaning of life. No answers, but lots of interesting ruminations. As my new friend Al says, "The nice thing about life is that it gives us something to do!"

CHAPTER 14

THE LAST WALTZ?

CHRISTOS

"Oh my soul, bless God. From head to toe don't forget a single blessing! He forgives your sins every one. He heals your diseases every one. He redeems you from hell saves your life! He crowns you with love and mercy a paradise crown. He wraps you in goodness beauty eternal. He renews your youth you're always young in his presence!"
Psalm 103 (Peterson: The Message)

W hat do you see when you look up into the pulpit on Sunday mornings? Saint, sinner, sage, slick, stooge, savior? He/she is all of those things, being human and all. But somehow God uses these strange creatures to proclaim the Word of Grace to all who will listen and believe.

Ben Franklin said of the early American evangelist, George

Whitefield, the words proceeding from his mouth were akin to beautiful flowers growing out of a muddy pond. I must have provided pretty good compost with my sermons.

I ended my ministry as I began. We "built" a new church from scratch. It stands on a high hill near Lake of the Pines. When I retired a new pastor was assigned. It is prospering and growing and enjoying all the epiphanies I had hoped it would. To paraphrase St. Paul, "Someone planted, I watered, and God gives the growth."

There were steep hills and soothing valleys. It was still somewhat like the above-mentioned ditty about Noah's Ark, but everything seemed to come together. The pastor is, after all, like St. Paul, a wounded healer.

I have finally reconciled the sacred with the secular, the Word with the Flesh, the Ideal with the Real. I know it's not "all about me," and it's not all about you. It's all about a Divine Influence that no one can discern fully. Love is born, lives, suffers, and dies, and lives again. Love brings its own glory, moment by moment. Nothing else does.

I have figured out for myself that my family, too, is the "Holy Family." Just as yours is. Nothing is more sacred to me than family gatherings, and special celebrations. We are all on our way to "Bethlehem," to be enrolled in the census for tax purposes. We are all "homeless" in this world, on the road to a home within. All my friends are sacred souls in my domain. All my enemies teach me humility. Someone said the only way to become humble is to be humiliated.

Was Mary holy? Was Joseph holy? Was Jesus divine at birth, or later when the Spirit descended on him at baptism, as some scholars propose. These are the kinds of things scholars have pondered for centuries. Let them ponder.

Jesus is still majestic with or without the miracle stories, and his love still transcends all others as he recruited misfits and hung on the cross. I find miracles and marvels every day in my experience, and in the lives of others. "You shall know the truth, and the truth will set you free."

My latest gift from Mother Nature is prostate cancer. I remembered Mark Twain's quip: "The Great Criminal" (his appellation for God) had designed a perfect body to give humans, and then added a disease to attack every possible part of that body. He postulated that Noah turned the ark around, after a few days adrift, to go back and pick up bugs from the carrion of the rotting animals, so that he could board two of each of those, to plague the human race. In cynical astonishment Twain added, "Guess what these plagued human beings call this Divine Being: 'Our Father!'"

I networked among my friends who had gone through the same cancer diagnosis. Surgery, chemotherapy, seed implantation, or external beam radiation were my choices. I chose the latter.

I went for the prep. Like a lamb going to slaughter, I walked right into the prep room. What I thought would be a piece of cake turned out to be the most wretched five minutes I had ever spent. They called it a "simulation," so as not to worry you in advance. Lying on the table, this rather innocent looking nurse turned her back on me so I wouldn't guess what she was up to.

Then came reality. She turned around, went straight for my crotch, and with a horrible thrust inserted a tube down into my penis, without anesthesia. That was just the beginning. Down the tube came an injection of fluid. That was worse than the tube, but I was sternly informed that I shouldn't resist (as I was), for that would only prolong the agony.

The justification for this unique form of torture was that it enabled the nurse to "more precisely" mark the tattoos on my lower abdomen and hips for the radiological treatments. I learned later that a friend of mine, confronted with the same long tube dangling over his privates, leaped up from the table and said, "No thank you!" He was cured anyway. He got tattoos that worked without the "simulation." Smart man.

A few days later, as I lay on the glass table, bare ass, under the "Linear Radiological Accelerator" I found it a good time to reflect. I was staring up at the ceiling, while the huge, donut shaped beamer hovered and circled over me. This was a snap compared to the simulation. For two months of daily doses, I found myself at the mercy of three "radiological technicians," of whose credentials I had no knowledge. We live by faith.

Christ, if I hadn't had a prostate all these years, perhaps the holy life would have been a more simple challenge! I say "Christ," because the Gospel of John and some of St. Paul's letters assure us that all things are made by, through, and for Christ. I'm just questioning certain aspects of our God-given natures, as we all do.

The linear accelerator whirred and cleared its throat, circled back and forth, trembled near its mark, zoomed its beam on the target for thirty or forty long seconds. Then still in orbit, searched for another tattoo, and zapped away for another 45 seconds. I was assisted off the table, pulled up my pants, and left the hospital.

No discomfort, no sensation, no afterglow. Just a warm, fuzzy feeling in my crotch. I was on my way. It was the first of thirty-nine daily "treatments." I was "slip, slidin' away." But not yet. My PSA has gone down dramatically, so it appears I can be assured I will die of something else.

Have I been lucky? Yes. I understand that's a Greek concept having to do with the fates. Have I had good Karma going for me? It seems so, if I need Eastern religion to validate my good luck. Have I been blessed? Sure, if I call up my Biblical Judaic roots. Have I been chosen? I believe I have, if I want to invoke the Pauline doctrine of election.

I have gone from person to parson to person to parson to person. We are all pioneers and peripatetic pilgrims who can learn from one another.

If I were Episcopalian, I would be thinking about the blessedness of the next communion service. If I were Baptist, I would be glad I had been immersed. If I were Presbyterian, I would be grateful I was among the elect before time. If I were Catholic, I would take comfort in the authority of the church. If I were a Religious Scientist, I would know that the treasures of my heart and mind would manifest themselves sooner or later. If I were Pentecostal, I could hardly wait to be "slain in the Spirit" one more time. But as a "Maverick Methodist," I am serene in the confidence that God is love, large enough to include me.

It's not easy to pick one "faith" above the other. God must have a great sense of humor.

By "Amazing Grace" the Holy Spirit manages to wrap itself around each religious affiliation, and feed his sheep. Let alone, as Jesus said, the sheep "that are not of this fold." Does that include Muslims and Hindus and Buddhists and Confucians and ad infinitum? I'm sure of it. Our religious worlds tend to be so small. By faith, we all create our own envelope of being.

I think everyone has to discover for himself or herself how truly spiritual life really is. It is the spirit, after all, that shapes our character and our destiny.

"The soft droppes of rain perce the hard marble." (John Lyly, Euphues.) Faith is not a "belief" in creeds or a set of moral principles. Jesus did not like "God in a box." He thought outside the box, big time. Jesus is still the one Guy I trust. The "Sermon on the Mount" has never been surpassed.

Faith is a dynamic. Some people think they prefer romance. But what is romance, but spirit? Some prefer sports, but what is excitement, but spirit? Some prefer excellence in science, or research, or success. What are these in essence, but spirit? We love competition in every arena, and that "competitive spirit" is exactly as advertised.

From my point of view we are like fish in the ocean, looking for water, or birds looking for air in which to fly. The spirit of Christ, or true life, is all about us, here and now, alive and well, in us, and in all of creation. It is now and here that the Vertical converges with the Horizontal, heaven unites with earth, the divine in the human, and all is well in that moment.

It was e. e. cummings who said: "The end is in the beginning, and the beginning in the end, and all is always now." Jesus said, "If you give, you will get! Your gift will return to you in full and overflowing measure, pressed down, shaken together to make room for more, and running over." (Luke 6:38) There's no doubt I have received far more than I have ever given.

The brilliant "ancient" Catholic priest, St. Thomas Aquinas, is reported to have said,

"Na mo dat quod non habit," which I have been given to understand means "no man can give what he does not have."

I gave only that which I had been given.

The latest media thunderbolt is that wealth is a suppressant for happiness! "Nigerians are happier than Americans who rank seventeenth in the world in happiness!" Mexicans are the second happiest. No one disclosed the ranking system for joy. So I must be pretty happy. I will start saying to those who ask me how I am: "I am as happy as if I were dead broke!" J. Paul Getty said, "Money is good for the nerves." So I'm embedded in another paradox.

I will die without benefit of baptism by immersion, or "extreme unction" from a Catholic priest, or the enlightenment of the Buddha, or the nirvana of a Hindu. I go without the Pope ever kissing my ring, nor I ever having granted him an audience. But I did appreciate his poetry when he was just a guy. Holy smoke! Who will be next?

Winston Churchill was once asked, "Are you ready to meet your maker?" He replied, "Yes, but is my maker ready for me?" In John Burroughs poem, "Waiting," he says,

"I stand serene, knowing that my own will come to me. My heart shall reap where it has sown, and garner up its fruit of tears."

I have been a "wolf in sheep's clothing," and a "sheep in wolf's clothing." It matters not.

The "Sinister Minister" is all too human. I understand the root of the word "sinister" is a Latin word, which simply means "left." There is growing evidence that the early church fathers ruled out the "left" side of our psyches, because it implied women could have a divine role in the affairs of men. Women were sinister, so they said. Too much yin, not enough yang. So much major misery followed from one erroneous assumption.

So we have "HIS-story" vs. "HER-esy." We may never solve the "MY-stery."

We have to find the path, with the Spirit's help, all on our own. We are all like Father Abraham and Mother Sarah, "movin' on, we know not where."

Once upon a time I wrote

"SEA CREATURE"

My mind is a creature of the sea
Bound by the shores of infinity

Free to wander the fathomless depths
Or play in the shallows and mindless clefts

The currents and eddies can pull me down
Swirling in sorrows and anger and gloom

The waves can toss me and roll me about
And fill me with bitterness, envy, or doubt

Sometimes I find myself beached on the sand
Caught in the coral of what-might-have-been

Trapped in the shoals of a trite memory
Tangled in seaweed of dreary ennui

Then along comes a breaker of yet-to-be
The tug and pull of the deeps of the sea

Calling me out to the measureless zones
Wooed by the tide of eternity

So let me play in the Ocean of Now
Explore the deep caverns and murmurs below

My mind is a creature of the sea
Seeking the Thou that is hiding in me!

THE BEGINNING